To all connectors, especially to my sisters:

Marie Johnson
Regina Graham
Claudette Taylor

You have become world-class at drawing others in and making them feel significant.

To my dearest long-time friend, Becky King, who started my metamorphosis (remember what a mouse I was?).

To Connie Cooper, the friend who threw me a lifeline and held on for dear life.

To my dear, dear friend, Dr. Jimmie Jones, who was so certain I could do this.

Special thanks to Dr. David O'Keeffe and Dr. Charles Apple who first made me believe that just maybe I could write—if I had something to say.

Endorsements

Ever since we were little girls on the playground, we have felt the need to belong—to matter to someone outside our family circle. As Christian women, we still long for acceptance and understanding through connection with others. Through her insightful suggestions in *Bind Us Together*, Doritta leads us to fulfill this need for ourselves and for our Christian sisters.

> —Laurel Sewell, former first lady, Freed-Hardeman University, Henderson, Tennessee

Bind Us Together taught me that connections cannot be coerced, only chosen. Students are instructed to research what the Bible says about the need for connection with God and fellow Christians. God gave of Himself; we must do the same. I especially identified with the summary chapter, "Welcome Ties that Bind," which emphasized seeing all people as souls. God designed us for connection, which requires sacrifice of time and efforts in the best interest of others. The benefits of these sacrifices happen to be in our own best interest. God knows best!

> —Stephanie Vick, proofreader, Greenville, South Carolina

I studied these lessons with our ladies' class and wholeheartedly recommend each one to guide Christians in achieving better relationships. We learned how to foster meaningful fellowship. The book is a how-to guide for anyone who has ever struggled to find a place in a group.

> —Ann Dunnaway, chiropractor, Tuscumbia, Alabama

In an age of social media, deep meaningful relationships are rare. *Bind Us Together* meets a great need and teaches us how to make those connections, first with God and then with others. I love the discussion questions and actual ways to get involved!

—Rosemary McKnight, author of *Those Who Wait*, Henderson, Tennessee

As a ladies' Bible class teacher, I'm always searching for challenging material to promote growth. After reading *Bind Us Together*, I am eager to present these ideas of developing the awareness of others! Disconnection is a very real problem in many congregations. We often focus only on familiar, comfortable acquaintances. Shame on us! Not only does this book make us aware of this issue; it gives us very sound, definite steps leading toward unity. There is no such thing as an unneeded Christian. "Bind us together with cords that cannot be broken," we often sing. What a powerful book, full of tools for strong ties of love!

—Becky King, elder's wife and ladies' Bible Class teacher, Anderson, Indiana

I really appreciate how Doritta uses Jesus as our example and compares our human connections with our connection to God. *Bind Us Together* shows how true connections enhance and benefit us, and others as well. Woven throughout are personal anecdotes and experiences, which let us know that she is real—she shares her apprehensions along with her successes. The reader will identify with the dimensions of connections in a journey that is rewarding and soul stirring.

—Dr. Marie Johnson, retired education professor, Freed-Hardeman University, Henderson, Tennessee

Contents

Chapter 1 Recognize the Need to Belong · · · · · · · · 9

Chapter 2 Open Your Eyes · · · · · · · · · · · · · 25

Chapter 3 See a Soul · · · · · · · · · · · · · · · · 41

Chapter 4 Adjust to Genuine Jitters · · · · · · · · · 61

Chapter 5 Open Your Heart · · · · · · · · · · · · · 77

Chapter 6 Stretch Out Your Hands · · · · · · · · · ·87

Chapter 7 Open Your Mouth · · · · · · · · · · · · ·97

Chapter 8 Share Kind Deeds · · · · · · · · · · · · 107

Chapter 9 Meditate and Evaluate · · · · · · · · · · 121

Chapter 10 Jump into the Deep End · · · · · · · · · 131

Chapter 11 Avoid Faulty Connections · · · · · · · · 145

Chapter 12 Plug into the Main Power Source · · · · · 153

Chapter 13 Welcome Ties that Bind! · · · · · · · · · 169

Works Cited · · · · · · · · · · · · · · · · · · · 176

Recognize the Need to Belong

Julia was supposed to be working on a study of the "one another" passages for her Sunday morning Bible class, but she just couldn't stop thinking about something Viola had said in Bible class the night before. Where did Viola get that thought she shared? Why had it stuck in Julia's mind? Viola had observed, *Sometimes the Lord calms the storm. Sometimes he lets the storm rage and calms his child.*

Viola seemed to live a storm-free life. With two children doing well in school and being generally liked by everyone, and with a husband who spoke kindly to her, Viola was always smiling, always patient. *What does she know about storms?* Julia wondered.

As she chewed on her pencil, Julia realized she didn't really know Viola, even though the two women chatted frequently and had many opportunities to be together. Julia mused, *Viola always makes me feel valued. But now that I think about it, I don't know anything about her. She never talks about herself or shows any side of herself except the giving, listening side. She seems to live the "one another" passages for others, but no one can live them for her, because she doesn't seem to need prayers or comfort or help with burdens—she doesn't seem to have any burdens.*

Julia's thoughts stalled for a moment or two. Then: If Viola wasn't busy in the congregation, she would be invisible. We see her because she's always there, but we don't really see her; we see what she does.

Bind Us Together is not about friendships. It is about connections—like being connected to the internet or like connecting to a caller on the phone. You can be in the same room with a computer that has internet access, but until you take the steps to connect, the internet remains only an opportunity. You may dial someone on the phone, but until that person picks up and says hello, the telephone remains only a tool, a prop, or a paper weight. It takes two to make a connection. While connections can lead to friendships, we can also be connected and have relationships without those relationships being BFFs (best friends forever).

Paths Crossing vs. Connecting

This book will help you distinguish between "being adjacent" and "having a connection," like the difference between tossing a magnet onto a wooden table and tossing it onto a metal surface. On the wooden table the magnet is merely adjacent, but on a metal surface it connects. On any given day we may be adjacent to others without being connected to them. Like tiles on a Scrabble board, we can be adjacent and productive, but not connected. Connection requires a knowledge and understanding of each other. In the body of Christ we need to be like the magnet looking for metal surfaces with which to connect or the metal surface to which a magnet may connect. This book is about how to transform an encounter into a connection.

Dissolve the Dividing Lines

Writing is hard work for me, but I am compelled to write because I have something to say. I need to say it because I have learned that connecting is vital. Contrary to popular belief, relationships don't just happen. Most of the time, true bonding develops only if we initiate and follow through. I am convicted to share these lessons because of personal experiences and the experiences of others in some congregations. Some smaller congregations contain a majority of members who are kinfolk—many "McCoys" and a few "not-McCoys." Walk into the auditorium and stop behind that last pew. You can almost see the dividing line. The McCoys and the not-McCoys never connected with each other, never blended into one body. These churches often become extinct.

> **Connection** (from Latin. *connex onem* "to fasten together, to tie, join together"): A line of communication between two points.
> **Synonyms:** Acquaintance, agent, ally, association, contact, friend, go-between, intermediary, kin, kindred, kinship, mentor, messenger, network, reciprocity, relation, relative, sponsor.

I know of two congregations with opposite situations. One outgrew the church building; the other was small in number and could barely afford the payments on a large building. The two congregations made an agreement to use the same building at the same time. I won't use the word "merge" because they didn't. People in town gossiped about the battles that went on in the building, in the parking lot, and in business meetings. The new congregation housed four hundred members. Within a few years, it numbered fewer than a hundred. The two never merged; they never became one.

On the other hand, consider the thriving congregation whose members loved and supported each other. They were a family looking out for one another. One day they became convicted that they needed to look outward and serve the community. They went to work with a will, establishing clothing giveaways, a food pantry, and a counseling service. It was beautiful! Then they became "fishers of men," and they were good at it. They were catching "fish," throwing them into the boat, and then catching more and throwing them into the boat. The newly caught fish either learned to live in abandonment on the bottom of the boat or they died. And we all know that there is not much water in a boat. The old members spent little or no time showing new converts their place in the body and how to fulfill it.

Keep in mind that in each of these dividing line examples, women composed approximately two-thirds of the group.

Times are changing, of course, but historically, women are best at building relationships. How does that fact make a woman significant in linking the members of a congregation to each other?

Most congregations have members who are not seen because they enter the assembly at the last minute and leave immediately after the last amen. Is it because the local church provides no opportunity to connect during the time they should most look like a body? Other members participate in various programs of the church, so we know them for what they do, but we cannot practice the "exhort, comfort, and bear one another's burdens" commands because they close themselves away from opportunities to be served. They don't share their needs.

I am motivated to write because I've seen too many Christians who have no bond with the group wander away. Their

12

backsliding is not necessarily because they have lost their faith; they may still believe in God. But perhaps they failed to experience communion with fellow Christians and with the Godhead— the very reason God directs us to assemble, to be an active part of the body of Christ.

I'm writing these lessons in hope that you will recognize yourself as a significant part of the body of Christ. I pray that you will see the following traits in your future:

- *Look at and listen to your neighbors.* See them. Hear them. Recognize their greatest need is for Christ. Be his eyes, ears, hands, and feet.

- *Look at and listen to your brothers and sisters in Christ.* You do not have to become best friends with everyone you meet. No one has the time, energy, or resources for that. What you do need to do will cost you a little time, a little thought, and all your love for God—all your appreciation for what he has done for you.

How Is Your Vision?

I pray that this study will provoke you to think about the invisible ones in your congregation. Are you, as a branch, firmly connected to the Vine? Do you see the church as a body in which each member is significant and needs to be firmly connected?

There aren't many original thoughts in my head, so don't count on me to tell you a lot of new methods. Rather, I am sharing experiences gathered from others along the way and from my own trials and errors. So far I have lived in nine states and one foreign country. Spending so much time among strangers, I recognized my urgent need for learning how to bond with others. So every time I heard an idea, saw a successful connection developing, read a relevant book or article, or saw an action demonstrating a bond forming, I noted it and dropped the idea into a file folder. The book you hold in your hands is a result of that gathering. I give credit where possible. If there is something here that I learned from you and did not give you credit, I welcome a note from you saying, "I taught you that!" Truly, I would love the connection!

Why might you be interested in this study? Perhaps you are new to a community or organization and you need to make new friends and don't know how to start. Or perhaps you have been in a group for a long time and often think about reaching out to people you barely know, but don't know how or you have been afraid to or you just haven't made the commitment. Perhaps you are nervous around strangers and are hoping to find a "how to" list of things to do. Most importantly, you might be convinced as Paul was: "knowing the fear of the Lord" you wish to persuade others (2 Corinthians 5:11). There are many reasons to invest in learning to forge links with others.

Without connections, after the day's work is done, life can be lonely. Who comes to mind that might be receptive to developing a bond with you?

We live such busy lives we hardly have time to say hello to those we meet, much less connect with them in a meaningful way. How is this contrary to God's way?

There is so much stimulation in our lives that it is difficult to focus on a single matter for more than a few minutes. We must learn to concentrate on those in need. Name one way to be more aware of the needs of others.

In our economy, many people work two jobs to care for their families. When they finally grab a few minutes free of urgent tasks, they are usually too tired to reach out to strangers. How and where can a busy worker take time to form a kinship with members of the body?

Some people are ashamed of their past. They believe anyone who gets to know them will reject them, so why should they bother making an effort. How can you meet their needs and become a person they can trust?

Job changes and relocations bring us to new communities, cultures, and circumstances, and we are fearful. Does that fear excuse us from making an effort? How can we learn to bond with others?

Every happening, great and small, is a
parable whereby God speaks to us, and
the art of life is to get the message.

–Malcolm Muggeridge, British Journalist

Mentor Material

Connecting might be easy for you. You might be comfortable with
all the assignment choices provided in these pages. Wonderful!
But you might find some of the assignments out of your comfort
zone. Don't worry. Just do what you can. As with yoga, any effort
at all is productive. Participating outside of class and in class
will bless you and others. Discussing or sharing your thoughts in
class has a twofold benefit.

1. Discussion helps others understand their own experience a
   little better.

2. Sharing will benefit you in clarifying the process in your own
   mind.

Sometimes you don't know what you think until you say it
out loud. No one is born knowing everything. Don't we all learn
through reading, watching, and hearing? When you share your
experiences with others doing this study, you are mentoring.
Thank you for being a mentor.

Growth Requires Focus

To get better at anything, you must focus. Your assignments will
provide an opportunity to focus on seeing and hearing the souls
around you. Perhaps you have been thinking about getting to

know visitors and new members. Let the ideas in these lessons help you focus.

Having moved many times in my life and having left good friends behind, I learned again and again how to create and build new friendships. Some find it easy to initiate conversations and relationships, but for me it is not easy. However, without the bonds of friendship, life is barren. In the past, while waiting for "adjacent" to become "connection," I became discouraged and occasionally depressed.

Learn to lean on your divine connection when you feel discouraged. Remember, there's a balance. Continue to strengthen your relationship with God as you cultivate new human relationships. Both connections are vital for good mental, emotional, spiritual, and physical health. Let the word of God inspire you: "Jesus kept increasing in wisdom and stature, and in favor with God and men" (Luke 2:52 NASB).

Like everyone else, I feel the need of relations and friendship, of affection, of friendly interaction, and I am not made of stone or iron, so I cannot miss these things without feeling a void and deep need.

–Vincent van Gogh, Dutch Painter

A Place to Belong

We want to belong. We crave companionship and intimacy. Experiences of being loved stay with us. They affect who we are and who we become. When others love us and we love others, we are in a win-win situation.

Write your thoughts about the obvious bond of Jesus with Lazarus, Martha, and Mary. As with all relationships, theirs must have begun with seeing and hearing each other. Make up a story about their very first meeting.

Write Proverbs 18:24. How may a friend give more of a "place to belong" to you than a brother?

I believe the greatest gift I can conceive of having from anyone is to be seen by them, heard by them, to be understood and touched by them.

–Virginia Satir, American Psychologist and Educator

Do you sometimes feel totally alone? The more you know about that kind of moment, the better you can handle it when it occurs again—and it will occur again. Describe one of those moments, using the following questions, but don't limit your description to these points.

🎵 What time of day or night did it occur?

🥾 What happened just before the moment?

🥾 How did you react to the feeling?

 While your experience is fresh in your mind, describe how it feels to share a bond of friendship.

Eye-Openers

Some years ago, Karen Mains wrote an article for *Today's Christian Woman* magazine: "Falling in Love with Scripture Again." She addressed those who read the Bible but get nothing out of it. She suggested we "give [ourselves] time and space for falling in love" with scripture. She recommended that the readers choose "one passage and spend weeks, months, maybe even a year in it." I said earlier that everything I know I learned from someone else. The quote above stands alone on a notecard in my manuscript folder. However, because I took her advice, I can recall the gist of her plan:

1. Choose a passage.

2. Read it for several weeks, sometimes aloud.

3. Use inductive reasoning to determine the writer's point. (It might be a promise, an intention, an example of behavior, or an illustration of God's character.)

4. Write down the passage.

5. Memorize the passage.

Why did I drop this note on studying scripture into my working folder on connecting with others? And why am I sharing it with you? Because the principles of learning to love the scripture also apply to forming bonds with each other.

🪶 Choose someone as a potential friend, and give yourself time and space for "falling in love." How do you get to know that person over time?

🪶 Remember important bits of information such as birthdates and children's names. Make a note of them if you need to. Writing something down is not cheating. Think about what is happening between you and the person with whom you are trying to connect.

What to Expect

Chapters 5 through 12 are designed specifically to train you to take notice of everyone in your congregation or in your community. Allow at least a week per assignment. Don't choose a different person for each assignment. Limit your interactions to a few people, no more than three or four for the entire study. The purpose is to connect with them—not to bump into them and then bounce off.

Each chapter presents three or four options. You may choose one or all of them. You will be asked to think before you act and again after you have completed the assignment. After the fourth assignment, you will be asked to evaluate the progress. Then you will spend some time at the end of the study to consider the results and think about your future plans.

Be aware of results as you complete the assignments. You will be asked to discuss your feelings in class or with a trusted friend. Meditating and discussing will help you internalize what you are learning. Then you will become more comfortable in reaching out. Becky Horton, in a presentation at a Southern Africa Bible College lectureship, said, "Thinking out loud helps us disentangle our thoughts." This material provides questions to get you started thinking, and you will be asked to think out loud.

Sharpen Your Skills

If you don't seem to have difficulty making connections but are part of a class using this book, your life-experiences should make it easier to choose assignments and to complete them. It might also be easier for you to share with the class the significance of what happens between two people in the initial stages of friendship. Your experiences are unique, but your comments might trigger another's understanding. God bless you in this opportunity to be supportive of someone who is learning to include others rather than to pass them by.

The purpose of this study is to help each student learn to develop her own bonds. World-class connectors will be encouraged to recognize their success and understand why they are successful. I pray that you will sharpen your plug-in skills and share your experiences. Remember, sharing helps to clarify thoughts. If you have mastered the art of relationship building, I pray that you will share your experiences and be a mentor.

While you are busy choosing a person with whom to connect, you might find that someone in the class has chosen you. What a blessing that can be! Please be open and available. Be responsive. Be prayerful. Thank you for receiving so that others may practice connection. Receiving is an excellent opportunity to focus on kinship from the perspective of receiving. I wish I could be there to hear your discussions!

 ## The Most Important Connection

Ask God for help as you work your way through this book. Commit to being genuine, discreet, and open for the long haul. This book may be a 13-week class or a few days' reading, but relationships are an ongoing process. This book is not written by an expert, so you will probably be able to expand on the thoughts and suggestions made in it. If you think of a better idea, use it! Let this study be only the starting place for you.

Begin with prayer for yourself and for those to whom you will be reaching out. At this moment you may not know who these people are, but God knows. Pray for yourself and for them. Begin to pray for those who will try to initiate a connection with you. As I developed the manuscript for this book, I prayed for you as one who is reaching out and also as one to whom others are reaching out.

> Let us then with confidence draw near to the throne of grace, that we may receive mercy and find grace to help in time of need (Hebrews 4:16).

 ## Shine Your Light

Are you one of the few people who doesn't need this book? Creating a bridge appears to be easy for some people. You will find yourself in some of these lessons, because part of what I have learned came from watching you. Perhaps some of the assignment choices will not seem uncomfortable to you, and you may even wonder, "Why do we need to think about creating connections with others?" Here are two reasons:

1. You will find it easier to focus on someone in your congregation you have not noticed before.

2. You will have an opportunity to share your knowledge, experience, and enthusiasm for meeting and greeting others.

On the other hand, you might be one of many people like me who feel disconnected but find it very difficult to start the process. You may begin this process of connecting immediately by listening to the announcements during the next assembly. Take note of people and their needs. For example, Diane Smith is scheduled for surgery on Tuesday. Do you know Diane? If not, your first step is painless. Put a name to a face and a face to a name. Begin to see souls. Identify Diane and begin to pray for her.

Regardless of your past attitudes about meeting someone for the first time, you can let your light shine during this quarter of study! Don't hide it under a bushel.

If the effectual fervent prayer of a righteous
person avails much, what does silence do?
—Unknown

Find a scripture that motivates you to take the first step in making sure all members of the body of Christ are included.

It is one of the beautiful compensations
of this life that no one can sincerely try to
help another without helping himself.
–Charles Dudley Warner, American Author/Essayist

Open Your Eyes

2

Viola spent her days, and most nights, happily serving her husband, their children, and the church in every way she could. After all, she was the preacher's wife. Breakfasts and dinners were sit-down meals around the table where news was exchanged. She taught Bible class on Sundays, Tuesday mornings, and Wednesday nights. She created bulletin boards. Members of the congregation often dropped by for visits.

Through most days Viola wore a smile. But nights? Well, nights were often difficult. While she was up and working, she worked "as unto the Lord" and was content. Anyone watching her probably thought she was sailing through life with no problems. But at night Viola faced the reality that she was alone. There was a secret in her life she dared not share. She believed that if people knew her secret, life would be unbearable. The only way to be sure you don't tell a secret—or let something slip that can give an attentive person a clue—is to keep quiet. So Viola kept quiet. She became an excellent and sympathetic listener but shared nothing beyond recipes and hobbies. So at night she cried because she was surrounded by good people but was totally alone.

The need to be connected is not something we made up. Don't think you are selfish because you need others. God wants us to be available and bonded to each other; he hardwired us with that desire. Your Creator knows you. He knows what you need.

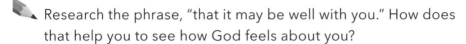

Research the phrase, "that it may be well with you." How does that help you to see how God feels about you?

Read Psalm 139. Describe several ways that God is connected to you.

What Does God Say about Our Need for Each Other?

1. He began with two people when he created the human family, because "it is not good that the man should be alone" (Genesis 2:18).

2. He wants us to be connected because "two are better than one, because they have a good reward for their toil" (Ecclesiastes 4:9).

3. We have further confirmation that God wants us to be connected when we look at the following "one another" scriptures:

   ♪ "Pray for one another" (James 5:16).

   ♪ "Confess your sins to one another" (James 5:16).

   ♪ "Love one another" (1 John 3:11).

🎵 "Exhort one another" (Hebrews 3:13).

🎵 "Encourage one another" (1 Thessalonians 4:18).

🎵 "Bear one another's burdens" (Galatians 6:2).

🎵 "Show hospitality to one another without grumbling" (1 Peter 4:9).

🎵 "[Submit] to one another out of reverence for Christ" (Ephesians 5:21).

🎵 "Love one another with brotherly affection" (Romans 12:10).

The Body Is Connected

Our relationships should be so close that we can trust our friends enough to confess our sins to them, to exhort them, to receive exhortation from them, and to submit to them.

Another way we can know that being connected is part of God's plan is his use of the body as an illustration of the church:

> For just as the body is one and has many members, and all the members of the body though many, are one body, so it is with Christ. For in one Spirit we were all baptized into one body— Jews or Greeks, slaves or free—and all were made to drink of one Spirit. For the body does not consist of one member but of many. If the foot should say, "Because I am not a hand, I do not belong to the body," that would not make it any less a part of the body. And if the ear should say, "Because I am not an eye, I do not belong to the body," that would not make it any less a part of the body. If the whole body were an eye, where would be the sense of hearing? If the whole body were an ear, where would be the sense of smell? But as it is, God arranged the members in the body, each one of them, as he chose. If all were a single member, where would the body be? As it is, there are many parts, yet one body. The eye cannot say to the hand, "I have no need of you," nor again the head to the feet, "I have no need of you." On the contrary, the parts of the body that

seem to be weaker are indispensable, and on those parts of the body that we think less honorable we bestow the greater honor, and our unpresentable parts are treated with greater modesty, which our more presentable parts do not require. But God has so composed the body, giving greater honor to the part that lacked it, that there may be no division in the body, but that the members may have the same care for one another. If one member suffers, all suffer together; if one member is honored, all rejoice together. Now you are the body of Christ and individually members of it (1 Corinthians 12:12–27).

A Binding Design

Each part of the physical body has a function that serves the body as a whole. Eyes that see keep us from walking into things. Hands bring the food to our mouths. Feet take us where we want to go. The brain sends and receives signals that direct the whole body. Even our little toe, which can be quite unappealing, has the important job of helping us keep our balance. Body parts that cannot be seen—blood vessels, nerves, and internal organs—are as important as the parts that can be seen and which might be very attractive. Just as we need all our body parts to function at our best, the church and community need the input of all members to function at their best. Whether we recognize it or not, we are involved in the lives of others. If our eyes do not see, the body doesn't function at its best. If we don't recognize this analogy and function as God has designed us, not only are we not helping, but we are hindering the church and our communities as well. The Bible's analogy of the body illustrates that God designed us to be connected to each other.

Related: 1. Connected, associated. 2. Connected by kinship, marriage or common origin. 3. Having a close harmonic connection.

Consider this: The body of Christ is more than your local congregation. Just as the good function of your congregation depends on the spiritual health of each member, the function of the body depends on the spiritual health of each congregation.

What is your function in the body of Christ?

Why do you depend on others to function in a different capacity?

Seeing Paul's Connections

God wants us to bond with him and with each other. Notice how Paul showed the Christians at Colossae that they had a fellowship (connection) with Christians they had never met. Then we will examine scriptures that instruct us that God wants a relationship with us.

> Tychicus will tell you all about my activities. He is a beloved brother and faithful minister and fellow servant in the Lord. I have sent him to you for this very purpose, that you may know how we are and that he may encourage your hearts, and with him Onesimus, our faithful and beloved brother, who is one of you. They will tell you of everything that has taken place here. Aristarchus my fellow prisoner greets you, and Mark the cousin of Barnabas (concerning whom you have received instructions—if he comes to you, welcome him), and Jesus who is called Justus. These are the only men of the circumcision among my fellow workers for the kingdom of God, and they

have been a comfort to me. Epaphras, who is one of you, a servant of Christ Jesus, greets you, always struggling on your behalf in his prayers, that you may stand mature and fully assured in all the will of God. For I bear him witness that he has worked hard for you and for those in Laodicea and in Hierapolis. Luke the beloved physician greets you, as does Demas. Give my greetings to the brothers at Laodicea, and to Nympha and the church in her house (Colossians 4:7–15).

Circle the names of the people mentioned in the verses above. Then underline the characteristics of each. (For example: Tychicus—dear brother, faithful minister, fellow servant in the Lord.)

Why do you think Paul mentions these Christians by name?

How many are mentioned with no description?

Which person has the most traits listed?

How do you think the people in Colossae might have felt about all these people, even the ones they had not yet met?

Know *about* Him? Or *Know* Him?

A connection doesn't occur just because we have something in common with a sister or just because we sit next to her in an assembly. If we say nothing more than "Hi, how are you?" or

"How 'bout those Yankees?" we are adjacent but not connected. Connection requires knowledge and understanding of another person. Closeness with God requires the same thing: knowledge and understanding of who he is. It's not enough to know about him; we must come to know him.

A few years ago I began a Bible study with a friend by laying a foundation of faith in the Bible as the word of God. At the end of that short introduction, my friend said, "All this information is very interesting, but I just want to get to the feel-good stuff." Her religious friends praise God publicly and with great emotion for all the blessings in their lives. They project happiness in spite of troubles. My friend wanted that feel-good stuff. She did not understand that feeling joy during times of trouble is the result of knowing God, understanding details of his character, and being in agreement with him.

Why Am I Here?

"In the beginning, God created . . ." (Genesis 1:1). In the beginning of what? In the beginning of this bubble within eternity that contains us and time. What existed before "the beginning"? God and eternity. Nothing forced him to create, so why did he? He wanted offspring.

"Then God said, 'Let us make man in our image, after our likeness' " (Genesis 1:26). An image looks like the original, but it is not. We are like the original in that we talk, think, make things, care about people and things and goodness, are able to love and want to be loved in return, and want to be known. God, the original, thinks, talks, makes things, and cares about people, things, and goodness. He loves and wants to be loved in return. And he wants to be known.

1. *You are a part of God's gift to Christ.* God cared about his creation and wanted someone to keep it (Genesis 2:8–15). He created because he wanted to enjoy his creation (Genesis 3:8). Everything he created is his gift to Christ (Colossians 1:16), and it reflects God's love (John 3:35), which means you are a part of that gift, part of that love.

   Read Revelation 4:11 (KJV), in addition to the verses above. Does God need me? Why did he create me?

   How do the following verses emphasize what we mean to the Lord?

   Ephesians 2:10

   Titus 2:14

2. *God is love* (1 John 4:8). "Anyone who does not love does not know God, because God is love." This verse does not say, "God loves." It says, "God is love." Love is not one of his attributes in the same way that brown eyes are one of my attributes. Love is his nature. He is love. Because God is eternal, his love is eternal. His love came first. God told the Israelites,

   > It was not because you were more in number than any other people that the Lord set his love on you and chose you, for you were the fewest of all peoples, but it is because the Lord loves you (Deuteronomy 7:7–8).

The Lord loves you because he loves you. That love is forever. "I have loved you with an everlasting love" (Jeremiah 31:3). Can one love without expressing it in some way?

3. *God seeks a relationship* (1 Corinthians 13:5). Love "does not insist on its own way." God will not force his love on us or demand that we love him. True love requires free will. Because we can love, we can choose not to love. God created out of love, and he wants people who choose to love him to come live with him. What kind of relationship does God seek with us? Isaiah 54:5 says, "For your Maker is your husband, the Lord of hosts is his name." He wants an exclusive, close, faithful, care-giving kind of relationship with us, as a husband has with his wife. He also wants a Father-child relationship with us: "But to all who did receive him, who believed in his name, he gave the right to become children of God, who were born, not of blood nor of the will of the flesh nor of the will of man, but of God" (John 1:12–13). What a risk God took when he gave us a free will. He took the risk that, although he wants a relationship with everyone, few will choose a relationship with him. And the choice is ours.

4. *God will provide or make us able to survive, but that is not what he is about.* We can ask him to "give us this day our daily bread," but he wants to hear more about relationships. In Matthew 6:9–13 we find the example of prayer that Jesus gave us. Notice to what most of the prayer is devoted.

   ♪ "Hallowed be your name" reminds me of my relationship with him. He is the first and the most respected relationship of my life.

   ♪ "Your kingdom come, your will be done" reminds me that Christ's church is to be in my prayers.

🎵 "Forgive us our debts, as we also have forgiven our debt-
ors" reminds me that I'm talking about my relationships
with others, as well as with God.

🎵 "Lead us not into temptation, but deliver us from evil"
reminds me that God cannot be where sin is. Avoiding sin
is how I honor God and put him and his kingdom first.

We can conclude that the model prayer in Matthew 6 is
weighted toward our relationships.

5. *God wants to be known.* The book of Hosea is a parable of
God's love for his creation. "For I desire steadfast love and
not sacrifice, the knowledge of God rather than burnt offer-
ings" (Hosea 6:6). God desires to be known.

> Thus says the Lord: "Let not the wise man boast in his wis-
> dom, let not the mighty man boast in his might, let not the
> rich man boast in his riches, but let him who boasts boast
> in this, that he understands and knows me, that I am the
> Lord who practices steadfast love, justice, and righteous-
> ness in the earth. For in these things I delight, declares the
> Lord" (Jeremiah 9:23–24).

A relationship with us is important to God.

Read Genesis 3:8–10. What kinds of feelings might God have
experienced when his offspring, the companions he created,
hid from him and were afraid of him?

"But God shows his love for us in that while we were still sinners,
Christ died for us" (Romans 5:8).

According to Romans 5:8, how did God demonstrate your importance and that he wants to be connected to you?

"But when the fullness of time had come, God sent forth his Son, born of woman, born under the law, to redeem those who were under the law, so that we might receive adoption as sons" (Galatians 4:4–5).

Using Galatians 4:4-5, tell how God demonstrates your importance.

"As God said, 'I will make my dwelling among them and walk among them, and I will be their God, and they shall be my people'" (2 Corinthians 6:16).

How do you know that you are one of God's people?

There Is Room for You

In Ephesians 1 we learn that God had a plan for us before the world began. Based on this fact, the following narrative is a supposition of communication between The Word and Sovereign Lord, devising a plan: create and then redeem so deity has fellowship with the creation.

Once, before time began, God said, "We want offspring. Lots of them. Not creatures like the angels, but created beings who can choose us back. Offspring we can love and who will love us back." So God created Adam and Eve and he walked and talked with them every day. Meanwhile, the villain in our story, Satan, said, "Ha! I can't have this! No, I am going to mess this up!" And so he did. Adam and Eve sinned, and because God cannot be where sin is, he had to separate from them. God said to Jesus, "Do you still want them?" Jesus said, "Yes, I love them." God said, "Well, you are the only one who can save them." Jesus replied, "I'll do it." So they worked their plan to redeem their offspring, and when the time was right, Jesus gave up all that he was and all that he had with God to come to earth as a man to live a sinless life so he could redeem us from God's wrath. The omnipresent (all-present) one became small enough to live in a womb. The omnipotent (all-powerful) one who could command light to exist became subject to his Father, to his earthly parents, and to rulers of this world. The omniscient (all-knowing) one gave that up and had to learn to say "Light." The one who had no beginning and no end had to become human, and he had to die.

Jesus knew the job that was set before him. He knew he had to become human. He had to live a sinless life, to say no to temptation every time, which means he had to trust and obey God's laws perfectly, and he had to die on a cross (Deuteronomy 21:23; Galatians 3:13; Ephesians 2:16; Romans 6:23).

He gave up heaven and his equality as deity because he loves us. Giving is what love does. Jesus didn't lay those powers down to pick them up again when he returned to heaven. He gave them up. When you give something up, it's not yours any more. He came to earth to be a man. In the New Testament, he calls himself "Son of Man" more than he calls himself "Son of God." He loves us and is pleased to identify himself as one of us. When he had completed his mission, God was so pleased with him that he exalted him and placed him on a throne.

God—almighty God, creator of our universe—wants a relationship with you. Why should you want a relationship with him?

Finish this quote from 1 John 1:3:

"That which we have seen and heard we proclaim also to you, so that you too may have _____ with us; and indeed our _____ is with the Father and with his Son Jesus Christ."

What word from 1 John 1:3 above indicates your connection with God?

The Path for Relationship: Giving

The New Testament writers tell us that God wants a relationship with us so much that he sacrificed part of himself to make it possible. "For God so loved the world, that he gave his only Son, that whoever believes in him should not perish but have eternal life" (John 3:16), eternal life with God.

John reports Jesus' words: "No one can come to me unless the Father who sent me draws him" (John 6:44). He also reported that Jesus' death on the cross is the event that draws people. "And I, when I am lifted up from the earth, will draw all people to myself" (John 12:32).

God made the path for the relationship, and Jesus Christ told his disciples to teach this good news to the whole world: "Go into all the world and proclaim the gospel to the whole creation. Whoever believes and is baptized will be saved, but whoever does not believe will be condemned" (Mark 16:15–16). To have a relationship with God involves believing the gospel.

What is the gospel? Let Paul answer:

> Now I would remind you, brothers, of the gospel I preached
> to you, which you received, in which you stand, and by which
> you are being saved, if you hold fast to the word I preached to
> you—unless you believed in vain. For I delivered to you as of
> first importance what I also received: that Christ died for our
> sins in accordance with the Scriptures, that he was buried,
> that he was raised on the third day in accordance with the
> Scriptures (1 Corinthians 15:1–4).

Circle the gospel facts in the above text.

How does one obey the gospel facts? Circle the answer from
the text below:

> Do you not know that all of us who have been baptized into
> Christ Jesus were baptized into his death? We were buried
> therefore with him by baptism into death, in order that, just as
> Christ was raised from the dead by the glory of the Father, we
> too might walk in newness of life. For if we have been united
> with him in a death like his, we shall certainly be united with
> him in a resurrection like his (Romans 6:3–5).

Is Obedience the Same as Relationship?

When *faith* is used as a verb, it is always an action verb. It
announces something to be done. *Faith* may actually be defined
by a compound verb: "trust and obey." No matter how silly it
seems, having faith in the death, burial, and resurrection of Jesus
means we trust and obey God. We trust and obey his death,
burial, and resurrection.

We obey the gospel by turning from our old life of sin (put-
ting it to death), by being buried with him in baptism (immersed
in water), and by being raised from the water (resurrected) a new
person in Christ. When we do that, we are connected to God.

However, connection through obedience does not create relationship. Nor does obedience prove you have a relationship. Prisoners obey rules without having a relationship with the wardens. Sonship does not automatically create a relationship. How many parents do you know who do not have a relationship with their grown children? Nor does a wedding guarantee a relationship. A relationship requires more than obedience, DNA, or ceremony. Obedience to the gospel puts us in agreement with God. The more we know God and understand his character, the closer our relationship can be with him. Subsequently, obedience and submission and service naturally flow from a relationship.

> And by this we know that we have come to know him, if we keep his commandments. Whoever says "I know him" but does not keep his commandments is a liar, and the truth is not in him, but whoever keeps his word, in him truly the love of God is perfected. *By this we may be sure* that we are in him: whoever says he abides in him ought to walk in the same way in which he walked (1 John 2: 3–6, emphasis mine).

The test for knowing if I am in Christ, for knowing if I am connected to Christ and that I have a relationship with him, is not to count the number of things I obey—as if doing more good things than anyone I know obligates God to allow me into heaven. To know for sure that I have a relationship with God is to check the reason I do these things. Do I serve out of fear or obligation or to be able to blackmail God, or do I serve out of love and appreciation for what Christ has done for me? Is my service a reflection of my love for him and a reflection of my understanding of his love for me?

We know we are in Christ because our lives *reflect* our relationship with him. John tells us we can know by checking our actions to see if we are walking as Jesus did. That does not mean we should go out and select twelve apostles, change water to wine, and raise the dead. Walking as Jesus did means reaching out to others and drawing them to God the Father. Jesus didn't just point to God. He drew people to God. We must not just point to God; we must draw others to him. Walking as Jesus did means building relationships.

God wants us to open our eyes and our hearts to him: "If we love one another, God abides in us and his love is perfected in us" (1 John 4:12). God wants to be in us, to be a part of us. This connection is necessary to eternal life and spiritual productivity:

> Abide in me, and I in you. As the branch cannot bear fruit by itself, unless it abides in the vine, neither can you, unless you abide in me. I am the vine; you are the branches. Whoever abides in me and I in him, he it is that bears much fruit, for apart from me you can do nothing (John 15:4–5).

Are you connected to God? If so, how did that happen?

John 15:4-5 indicates that connection to God will make you productive. In what ways have you become more productive because of your connection with God?

A branch that does nothing but dangle from a vine is not healthy. You are a branch. Describe a healthy, sure, and strong connection to Jesus, the Vine. How fruitful is your branch?

See a Soul

3

Stella was sitting in her car in the church parking lot, trying to talk herself into going into the building. It was 9:15 and services had already started, but Stella was very discouraged. A recent college graduate, Stella had returned to her hometown to begin work in a leadership position at one of the largest companies in town. Life should be really good. But it wasn't. While away at college she had worshiped with one of the most loving groups of people in the world! She always left worship with a smile on her face and a song on her lips, looking forward to the next meeting. It was wonderful! But now she dreaded the assembly. People she had grown up with and thought were her friends now said cutting, hurtful things, with a laugh, of course, as if to say "just kidding." But it was apparent she was no longer a part of "the clan," and the remarks were dipping into her bucket seriously. As she sat in the car, her heart heavy, she wondered, *What am I going to do? Keep on attending here and be alone or create my own clan? Or, perhaps, try to find another congregation where I feel wanted? What if I make friends and bring them to this church? Will they be treated as I am?*

What a problem. If she stayed, did she have the strength and endurance—and skills—to change the environment? If she stayed, how would she keep her spirits up? What to do? "Dear God. What would you have me do? What will you help me do?"

In addition to the way it makes us feel, bonding with others is important because it helps us thrive. In the 1940s, medical doctors and sociologists began to study cases of babies' deaths in orphanages, even though they were well-fed, properly clothed, and had no known disease. They called this phenomenon marasmus disease, or a "wasting away." A study conducted by Dr. René Spitz, who observed babies in orphanages after World War II, was the beginning of our understanding that providing food and a clean environment are not enough for babies to thrive. Dr. Spitz reported that infant deaths were fewer when babies were held and talked to regularly. Virginia Satir, a social scientist and widely known as the "mother of family therapy," says we need four hugs a day to keep the blues away, eight for maintenance, and twelve to grow emotionally. Connections do more than make us feel good in the moment. We desperately need them to reach our potential.

Fire Up Your Brain!

MRI images show what happens in the brain during interpersonal interactions. The mid-brain is affected when interactions are unidirectional. On the other hand, the cerebral cortex, the area of the brain required to develop interpersonal skills, lights up when the interaction is reciprocal. Unidirectional (one way) interactions occur when a baby monkey is attached to a wire "mother," or when a child is attached to an object such as a blanket. The wire mother and the blanket give no response. They are just there. Attachments to non-responsives are rooted in insecurity or fear. Reciprocal attachments, as when a baby and her mother make eye contact along with happy noises, are not only comforting, but they also fire up the cerebral cortex in both the baby and the mother. At this moment the child is learning about her world: Is it safe? Am I loved? Do you see me? Am I important? Connections do more than make us feel good. They promote growth and development (Arredondo).

One man made the following statement in introducing the book of Colossians:

> Remove the head coach, and the team flounders. Break the fuel line, and the car won't run. Unplug the electrical appliance, and it has no power. Whether it's leadership, power, or life, connections are vital!

Most important, we need to connect with others in a caring way in order to have the opportunity to teach the gospel. It is an old quote, but forever true: "People don't care how much you know until they know how much you care."

Discuss the difference between unidirectional and reciprocal interactions.

Discuss these different responses:

🪶 When you feel appreciated by someone else.

🪶 When you have to interact with someone who is unconcerned with your feelings and values.

Created for Interaction

We sense the need for being close to others at a very early age, perhaps from birth. When that need is met, we begin to learn to join rather than avoid. We also learn that others value us and that others have value. When the relationship need is not met, we might believe that we cannot depend on or trust others. That causes us to withdraw and close ourselves off from others in order to protect ourselves. It further causes us to believe we are not valuable, not good enough to be loved.

> Man's deepest need is to love and be loved. But man is lonely, because he doesn't feel he can trust his goodness and his badness to his fellow men. So he wears a mask of superficial respectability. He tries to compensate for his loneliness by surrounding himself with labor-saving gadgets, prestige-producing possessions, and attention-absorbing amusements. But to no avail, for man is not a thing—he is a person—made to respond and be responded to; made for interaction and communication with other persons and with God (Thornton 5).

Whether or not the need for bonding was met from infancy, we must acknowledge this innate need, this God-given essential, and make the effort for ourselves and for others.

Soul on the Other Side

If you were drawing a scene involving a disconnected person, what would it look like? She might be inside a tremendously high and thick wall with no gate. There she is, the unique soul God created "unto good works," all alone, arms folded, seeing no one and being seen by no one. That is what it looks like, and how it feels is discouraging and depressing, and/or _____ (you fill in the blank with what it looks like to you). The trouble with being separated from people is that it makes us feel worthless or of little value—maybe even invisible.

It takes two people working together to make a connection. I can pray for you, give you gifts, and spend time with you, all without being connected to you. You may receive all these things from me without being touched. We remain adjacent to each other but not connected. But if I spend time with you, and you respond with an interest in me—the real me—by listening to and accepting the things that really matter to me, and I accept the part of you that you allow me to see, our magnet qualities activate. A conversation in which one person does most of the talking and the other listens attentively and asks appropriate questions might be gratifying and informative. Each might enjoy the conversation while it is happening, but later both may realize they are still not connected. Both have to open their gates.

There can be no relationship if there is a gateless fence around either conversant. If you are not bonding with others, maybe it's because you have closed yourself off. You might have to put a gate in the wall you have built around yourself. The nice thing about a gate is that you can open it to whom you wish. And you can open it if you wish and when you wish. But if you don't open it and allow someone to enter your space, you will remain alone all the time.

Have you ever felt invisible? Has it ever seemed that your voice was a whisper? Are you afraid, afraid of failure, afraid of making mistakes, afraid of being wrong, afraid of looking stupid? Disconnected people lack confidence. They are not sure they can make sound decisions. They often withdraw, in the hope no one will notice them; or they may become aggressive and misbehave so others will notice them. The main goal of the disconnected might be self-protection or it might be self-promotion. But either way, the disconnected live in a lonely, dark, dreary, and sad world.

Describe what you think or know it is like to feel totally alone?

When you feel alone, do you withdraw from others or do you become dramatic, hoping to be noticed? Describe your behaviors.

Do you know someone who appears to have shut herself off from the world? List reasons a person would do that.

Think of someone who never expresses her loneliness. She can be in a room full of people and feel lonely. Another person can be the only one in the room and not feel lonely. What makes the difference? Why would a person feel lonely while surrounded by people? How can a person be alone and not lonely?

Highlight or underline the descriptions of being connected that resonate with you:

Shared experience

Understanding without explanation

Wanting to know more

Going in the same direction

Makes me feel important

Know Her or Know *about* Her?

True connection is the difference between knowing about some-one and knowing someone. I know *about* Abraham Lincoln but I *know* my sisters. My sisters and I have shared experiences. We have a history of reaching out to each other, listening to each other, and caring for each other. We accept each other, flaws and all. As for President Lincoln, I know a lot about him, but we have never shared an experience. We aren't even adjacent. I am not adjacent to my sisters very often, but we are connected. When two people share happiness or sadness, courage or fear, anticipation or dread, a meal or a movie, whether with conversa-tion or companionable silence, they share a bond. A relationship involves sharing something.

When we share our feelings with others, we are less afraid of challenges and less afraid of other people. We are more con-fident, and we feel more valuable. We see ourselves as a part of a team, even if it's a team of two! We feel important to someone. We are more trusting and less afraid. Even Moses was bolstered when his brother, Aaron, joined his mission.

Discuss Andrew's running to find Peter and shouting, "We have found the Messiah" (John 1:35-41). What did Andrew's action say about their bond?

Being physically near someone does not necessarily result in connectedness. Electronic connection requires a conduit. Personal connection requires physical or emotional touch. Physical connection can be a pat on the back, a fist bump, or a hug. Emotional connection can be as simple as direct and lingering eye contact or verbally expressed agreement on a subject or action. Have you ever heard or observed something and turned to a friend, only to find her looking at you? Then, through eye contact, each of you knew the very thoughts of the other. Bingo! Connection. It requires two people working together with focus. The attention goes both ways.

Raise Your "Soul" Antennae

Soul-bonding requires reception. Send. Receive. That's a connection. Jesus was washing his disciples' feet in the upper room (John 13:3–17). When he came to Peter, Peter said, "You shall never wash my feet." Jesus replied, "If I do not wash you, you have no share with me . . . I have given you an example, that you also should do just as I have done to you." Part of the example in this story is that we should serve others, but another part is that we should receive favors from others.

Some will feel a connection to you without your knowing it. One of my colleagues at work invited me to a picnic with him and his girlfriend and, because of details not shared here, I assumed he was inviting me because he was inviting other office colleagues and didn't want to hurt my feelings. I declined.

I found out on the following Monday that I was the only one from the office who had been invited, and it was not actually a picnic. It was my friend's outdoor wedding. When I told him I was sorry I had declined, he said, "That's okay," in a way that let me know it was not okay. He was very disappointed. What a lesson! I was important to him but had not received his attempts to connect with me. If someone invites you, assume it is because that person wants to be with you. Go. Be available. Receive their signal to connect.

Relationships are about sharing, not about helping others. Helping can insult by making one person feel superior and the other person feel inferior. Lending a hand can be confused with "setting someone else straight" and can actually keep you from becoming connected. The assignments in this book may seem to be about helping others, but the goal is to use the assignments to help you associate by providing an opportunity to focus on the following traits:

- Listening to others
- Recognizing intrinsic qualities, rather than outward appearances
- Allowing others to be themselves by providing them a safe space
- Valuing others as God created them

Visible and Valuable

My prayer is that the assignments will help us do for others what God's love does for us. God's love enables us to trust and obey, grow up, learn who we are and what we are capable of, and develop a relationship with him. Our friendships should help us learn to trust each other and to be trustworthy, grow spiritually, develop confidence and courage, and develop a supportive and caring family of God.

At no time during this study should you spend time and energy trying to set someone straight, as Job's friends did. Your aim will be to accept, understand, and permit.

> God does not will that I should fashion the other person according to the image that seems good to me. He made that person in his image. I can never know beforehand how God's image should appear in others (Bonhoeffer 93).

Throw away your cookie cutter and meet people where they are. Remember, while we were sinners, Christ died for us. Why should your sister have to be perfect before you befriend her?

The aim of this book is to provide acts of love whereby you may stand ready to encourage others as they draw closer to God and reinforce good traits as they catch a glimpse of themselves— who they are and what they have to offer. These actions of love will convey to your sister that she is visible and valuable.

We were made to give and receive, to help and to be helped, to encourage and to be encouraged. Our nature requires a tie to faithful others.
—Leroy Brownlow, Author

Our study involves more than reaching out to others. It is also about receiving. "Can you hear me now?" Give and receive. Let's work on connectedness. Let's get to know others on a deep and authentic level. Let's create an emotional bond with others and practice receiving. Nevertheless, some additional benefits you may discover are better relationships, spiritual growth, heal- ing, leadership skills, and better physical and emotional health.

Describe a time when someone reached out to connect with you, and you did not understand their attempt until later.

Describe a time when someone gave you advice to "set you straight." Did you receive the advice graciously or did you resist it? All of us, at least occasionally, need this kind of advice. What would make the difference in the way we receive this kind of advice?

Describe a time when someone expressed an appreciation for you.

Did the attempt to set you straight or the attempt to show appreciation draw you closer to the other person and to God? Which of these attitudes will you choose for the assignments provided later in this book?

Put Power in Front of Your Eyes

David E. Arredondo, in his video, "Human Connectedness and Attunement," provides the following evaluation list and suggests that we put it on a card, laminate it, carry it in our pocket, and pull it out when we meet someone new so we can assess her connectedness potential. Review his list to evaluate your own potential for bonding. Professor Arredondo says that to be able to connect with others, we need these characteristics:

- Emotional availability
- A degree of flexibility
- Consistency
- A range of emotion
- Capacity for general playfulness
- Initiation of affectionate interaction
- A sense of humor
- Patience

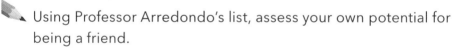

Using Professor Arredondo's list, assess your own potential for being a friend.

- Am I emotionally available or am I withdrawn?
- Have I isolated myself emotionally?
- Is my sense of what is acceptable rigid or flexible?
- Am I obsessive-compulsive about my time and opinions, or am I somewhat flexible?
- Am I relatively consistent regarding my values and standards?

Be Consistent and Trustworthy

Consistency allows others to be able to predict how you will behave in a given circumstance. Consistency makes it easier for others to decide whether or not they can trust you with their "real" selves.

1. Do you feel and can you express a range of emotions, or do you feel only anger or sadness, or do you laugh inappropriately?

2. Do you have a capacity for general playfulness, or is it "all work and no play" for you?

3. Can you initiate affectionate interaction, or are you closed and withdrawn?

4. What is your connectedness potential?

Trust: Total confidence in the integrity, ability, and good character of another.

The word *trust* is not in the previous list, but if we don't trust others, how can we be emotionally available? Without trust, we are inflexible and will rarely if ever initiate affectionate interaction. Trust is the foundation to all close interpersonal interactions. Make sure you are trustworthy. Otherwise you'll miss out on stable relationships.

If you have difficulty trusting others, choose assignments in chapters 4–12 that don't require you to disclose too much of yourself. Start with non-threatening assignments. As you succeed, your levels of trust should grow. If you are more trusting, keep in mind that some of your contacts might not trust you or anyone else. Be kind, patient, and non-threatening. Don't be forceful; do be trustworthy. Do not press for disclosure.

Life experiences teach us that it is impossible to connect with everyone. Even Jesus was not popular with everyone! Do you experience times when you don't like you? I know there are times when I don't like me. So not everyone will like me all the time, and some will not like me any of the time.

Some people don't appreciate pearls. They
just want a quarter for an arcade game.

–J. Jones

Is the Enemy Me?

There have been times when it seemed I was not connected to anyone! I wondered, "Is there something wrong with me?" The answer was, "Perhaps."

- Perhaps I needed to be more flexible or more patient.

- Perhaps I needed to initiate rather than to wait for someone else to reach out to me.

- Perhaps my response was not appropriate.

- Perhaps I responded with advice instead of sympathy.

- Perhaps I could connect more often with others if I would pat their backs instead of telling them what they should have done or should do.

- Perhaps I should never miss a good opportunity to shut up.

A little girl returned home late from a play date with a neighborhood friend. When Mother questioned her tardiness, the child said, "I would have been home sooner, but Darcy's favorite doll got broken."

"Did you stay to help her fix the doll?"

The little girl replied, "No. I helped her cry."

How do you measure up as a connector? List your strongest attributes. How will you improve on your weaknesses?

Discuss how trust or a lack of trust impacts our relationship potential.

Comment on the quality of trust in the woman of Proverbs 31.

 ## Dipper and Bucket

Some time ago, I think the 1970s, I heard of a book, *How Full Is Your Bucket?* by Dr. Donald O. Clifton. Popularity of this book has been revived in recent years and has been used a lot in public schools. You may be familiar with it. I don't have a copy of the book but below is the gist of an excerpt of it from my memory.

Everyone has an invisible bucket and dipper. The contents of the bucket determine how we feel about ourselves and others and how we get along with people. Have you ever experienced a series of very favorable things that made you want to be good to people? When that happens, your bucket is full to overflowing. You have a sense of well-being, a sense of worth.

Your sense of worth can be filled in many ways. When a person speaks to you, recognizing you as a human being, your bucket is filled a little—even more if you are called by name, especially if it is the name you like to be called. If you are complimented on your dress or on a job well done, the level in your bucket rises. It also rises when you make a mistake and a friend says, "I have had that happen to me. Let me give you a hand." There must be a million ways to raise the level in another's bucket: writing a friendly letter, remembering something that is special to someone, knowing the names of someone's children, expressing sympathy for loss, giving a hand when someone's work is heavy, taking time for conversation, or, perhaps more important, just listening. When a person's bucket is full of emotional support, she exudes warmth and friendliness.

But remember, this is a theory about a bucket and a dipper. We also have invisible dippers. Others can dip from our buckets and we can dip from theirs. That too can be done in a million ways. Think of the times when you have made a mistake and feel terrible about it, only to have someone put the icing on the cake by reminding you of it. Also, when you are ignored, when you are interrupted while talking about something important to you, or when you are not invited to a party that includes your friends, others are dipping into your bucket. You are allowing them to diminish your sense of self-worth. And when you do these things to others, you dip into their buckets. Most of the time, buckets are emptied by people who don't really think about what they are doing.

The story of our lives is the interplay of the bucket and the dipper. Everyone has both. The unyielding secret of the bucket and the dipper is that when you fill another's bucket it does not take anything out of your bucket. Actually, the level in your bucket rises when you raise another's bucket level. Conversely, when you dip into another's bucket, you lower your own bucket's level.

Discuss the theory of the bucket and the dipper. Include your thoughts about how your efforts to connect with others might fill buckets.

How will "filling someone's bucket" increase their sense of self-worth and help you connect?

 How does the concept of "filling someone's bucket" prevent sin? (Hebrews 3:13)?

Step out of Yourself

Interacting with people is not easy. Some will rub us the wrong way and some will reject us. Some cannot accept us because they have not learned to trust. Perhaps we are not on the same page because our own buckets are empty. But our efforts to connect are worthwhile. Our beginning efforts will be to fill the buckets of others and thereby fill our own—some to overflowing. For some individuals, it may be the only love they have received.

Your first step to offer friendship is not only difficult, it is risky. You have to be open with yourself and let another person in. And you can't be sure that she will be gentle when she comes in.

The level of your self-esteem (how full is your bucket?) affects what you say to yourself about yourself. Your confidence (again, your bucket) influences your willingness to serve another and change your own behavior. Connections are vital to your sense of personal satisfaction. And they fill buckets!

Sometimes we know we are lonely, but we don't know why, and we might not know how to change the situation even when we discover the reason for our loneliness. Loneliness results from a feeling of separation. Yes, our efforts to create kinship with others might be risky, but because God wants us to do it, expect a blessing.

What makes connections occur?

How may I be getting in my own way by being closed, passive, and untrustworthy?

Discuss the different results obtained when I (1) take responsibility for meeting my needs, or (2) require others to make me happy.

If I think of myself as loved, I can love and accept others. If I see myself as forgiven, I can be gracious toward others. If I see myself as powerful, I can do what I know is right. If I see myself as full, I can give myself freely to others.

—Kathy Peel, CEO of Family Manager Inc. and Author

Adjust to Genuine Jitters

oday was the day. Susan had been wanting to make a change in her worship experience for several months, and today she was going to throw her shoulders back and do something extremely difficult. When she recommitted her life to God a little over a year ago, the congregation had welcomed her back with open arms. But she continued to feel not quite like an outsider, but, well, on the fringe, on the outer edge of the group.

A few months ago when she realized she was slipping back into her old habit of sleeping in on Sunday morning, she prayed fervently for help to stay true to her commitment. During one of those prayers she expressed gratitude for the women who always chatted with her. Susan thought, *If I falter it won't be their fault. They invite me to participate in fellowship and work projects. They want to include me in everything.* Susan thought warmly of all their attempts to include her. *It doesn't seem reasonable for me to feel alone when they do so much to make me feel a part of the family.* Then she questioned herself: *Is it me? Am I holding back?*

Her thoughts leapt to Ann. During "talk time" between Bible class and assembly, Ann came

61

into the auditorium through the door farthest from where she liked to sit. Then as Ann made her way to her seat, she took the most circuitous route, greeting people, asking questions, and giving hugs or shoulder pats. The church loved Ann. She made everyone feel important.

Susan compared her own behavior to Ann's. *Hmm. All I do is show up and smile.* With an exasperated sigh, Susan thought, *But I'm not like Ann. She is so outgoing. I'm an introvert, and more than a little insecure! I can't do what Ann does!* And with that thought Susan jumped up and went back to work.

However, she couldn't stop thinking about Ann and about the question, "Is it me?" Soon it occurred to her: there is one Ann and one Susan. *I don't have to be Ann. I don't have to walk through the auditorium in front of everyone, speaking to everyone—horrors! But I can have a conversation with one person. Now, who could it be? I know! That red-haired girl across the aisle from where I usually sit. She asked for prayers last week. I will introduce myself and tell her how brave I think she is. I'll do it Sunday!*

So with a smile that hid her shyness and a step that over-came her timidity, Susan walked up as her friend-to-be was about to sit down. Touching her on the shoulder, she said, "Hi Rita. I prayed for you every day last week. It made a real differ-ence in my life, and I hope it did in yours as well."

For God gave us a spirit not of fear but of power and love and self-control (2 Timothy 1:7).

Have you been around babies who instinctively know how to connect with others? Aren't they totally charming? If things go well, they grow up being comfortable with strangers, assuming that everyone likes them and that the world was made just for them. Unfortunately for some, things do not go well, and they begin to assume a proportionate amount of distrust of people. We have the freedom to allow doubt and fear to be the ruling principles of our lives; however, if we abandon our trust in all humanity, we will miss out on some of God's richest blessings: friends.

Squishing the Jitter Bugs

- By choosing this study, you have indicated an understanding that some in the church, and perhaps even you, seem to be invisible or have not discovered their function in the church.

- By now you understand that using your eyes to see and your ears to hear is the first step. Good for you! Don't allow fear to make you hesitant. Hebrews 10:39 says, "But we are not of those who shrink back and are destroyed." Don't let Satan deter you. Don't shrink back. Forward is the direction for you!

- When you experience only a small amount of success and are tempted to hesitate or stop, read Galatians 6:9: "And let us not grow weary of doing good, for in due season we will reap, if we do not give up."

- Trying to connect with others is a very good thing, but it rarely occurs on the first attempt. Oswald Chambers says, "The [wave] that distresses the ordinary swimmer produces in the surf rider the super-joy of going clean through it." Give yourself a chance to be a "surf rider."

- If you are afraid to make connections because you think others won't like you when they get to know the real you, try reading *The Velveteen Rabbit*. The stuffed rabbit doesn't become real until he has lost an eye or nose, or until his fur is all rubbed off and stitching is coming undone.

Think about the kinds of friends you want in your circle. Don't you want friends who are "real" people? You know it's true. We may figuratively put on tons of cover-up, but underneath everything, we are all missing something or are continually re-stitching holes in our lives. Imagining that others won't like the real you is a lie Satan whispers to you in the dark of night. Don't listen to him.

You might need to work toward minimizing or eliminating your own negative self-talk or criticisms received.

Add to the following list some negative things you might say about yourself:

I am not as good as Julia.

I always say the wrong thing.

I am fat.

I am always late.

I am clumsy.

I am too young, too old, too dumb . . .

I am _____

What negative remark has someone said to you that might be holding you back?

To replace these negatives, add to the following list of positive thoughts:

I am not as good as I want to be, but I am better than I used to be.

My trust in God will help me have self-control (Galatians 5:19–24).

I am a valuable, one-of-a-kind soul, created by the most awesome Designer.

I am _____

You Don't Have to Remain Stupid

I enjoyed reading *All I Need to Know about Life, I Learned in Kindergarten*. It's a cute title, and the book has some great reminders. But I did not learn all I needed to know about people when I was five. I've learned a lot since—some of the same lessons over and over. I became more and more reserved before I finally decided to increase my knowledge about relationships.

When I was growing up, my dad continually said to my sisters and me, "Why don't you shut up? If you keep your mouth shut, people will think you are stupid. If you open your mouth, they will know you are."

My marriage relationship reinforced the concept that I must be stupid. Way down deep I didn't really believe it, but I closed myself off more and more lest people would discover for sure just how stupid I was.

At some point it occurred to me, "Okay, so maybe I am stupid. But I don't have to remain stupid." I started reading and building a personal library of interpersonal communication materials. Eventually I was awarded a bachelor's degree in the subject.

Dear reader, I am praying right now that you will rise above your fear, or whatever holds you back, and move toward making connections. We need more real people in this world—especially in the church.

As you reach out to others, follow God's example of connectedness:

🎵 God values you even though you are not the prettiest or the smartest or the richest kid on the block. Therefore, you should value others whether they are pretty or ugly, smart or not so smart, rich or poor.

🎵 While there are boundaries attached to a relationship with God, there are no strings attached to his love for you. It just is. Be prepared to set boundaries in any relationship that develops, but attach no strings to your love for others.

🎵 God values all people even if they are ugly or poor or mentally challenged. I may not know what significance you have in the body of Christ, but I know you are significant, because every part of the body is significant.

In other words, love because he first loved you and not for what you can get in return. The following quotes shed extra light on being motivated by love.

He that does good for God's sake seeks neither praise nor reward, but he is sure of both in the end.
—William Penn, Quaker Philosopher

You must therefore love me, myself, and not my circumstances, if we are to be real friends.
—Cicero, Roman Philosopher/Politician

The person who sees a chance to do a
good turn here and a little one there, and
shed a little light here and a little sunniness
there, has something to live for.

—Henry Drummond, Scottish Writer/Lecturer

Time for Action

Some people can "wing it" and succeed, but not me. I have to
read and research and analyze—everything. But once I have
an idea of how something could look or how a process can get
under way, my confidence excels. Carefully study this "Time for
Action" section. It will prepare you for the assignments in the
next eight chapters.

How is the following statement true? "We fall in love with those
who make us feel good about ourselves."

Think about someone with whom you have a special relationship. How do you feel about that relationship? What makes it a
connection?

Visualize an existing close friendship. As you answer the following questions about this relationship, keep in mind that these
traits will help you in completing the assignments in this book:

67

🎵 Write one reason that person is special to you.

🎵 What is the best thing about your relationship with that person?

🎵 What are two specific positive ways that your friend treats you that are different from the way she treats others?

As you make efforts to advance the cause of an all-inclusive congregation, keep in mind that what seems normal to you may not be normal for someone else. We grow up believing that our homes are normal, and we develop methods that become our standard ways of doing things.

Maybe you've heard the story about the young bride preparing her first Sunday lunch. She bought a ham, cut off the end of it, and put it into the oven. Her groom asked why she cut off the end. "Because that's how my mom cooked it," she replied.

The next time she saw her mom, she asked, "Why do you cut off the end of the ham?" Mom said, "Because that's how Grandma cooked it."

Then the bride took the question to Grandma. Grandma replied, "I don't know why you cut it off, but I cut it off so it will fit in my pan."

We relate, or try to relate, to others according to what seems normal to us, and eventually we discover two things: Our ways aren't the norm for everyone, and there are other equally valuable ways to do things.

🎵 You may be uncomfortable with some of your assignments in the following chapters, because they are not what you have done or the way you have done them. You may say, "Doing these things is just not me." And then you begin to feel hypocritical. Well don't! Hypocrisy is pretending to be something you are not and never intend to become. However, doing new things, or old things in a new way, is not hypocritical.

🎵 Each person is unique. There is only one you. Never has been, never will be another you. That is equally true of everyone around you.

🎵 Don't be put off by someone's differentness. Sometimes those differences add a dimension to the way they handle life, and understanding them could add depth to your life. Differences are not necessarily good or bad. They are simply differences. An example of different-but-good approaches to the study of God's word might be in family devotionals. One family has a formal bedtime devotional. Another family has conversations throughout the day about how God's word applies to daily living.

🎵 List examples of different-but-good approaches to doing things. Why do we need to recognize and incorporate new ideas?

🎵 Recognize the fact that there will be barriers to success. Some will be of your own making; some will be thrown up by the other person. The biggest barrier will be a lack of trust. You might have to build trust first.

🎵 Consider your strengths and weaknesses. In what kinds of environments are you comfortable? If you are uncomfortable in large groups, you will not want to walk across the room in front of people in order to introduce yourself to a stranger or to sit or stand near someone with whom you want to initiate a connection. Know yourself and be yourself, but be willing to get out of your comfort zone.

Where's Your Focus?

Sometimes fear is a result of having your focus in the wrong place. Remember what happened to Peter (Matthew 14:23–33). Verse 30 says, "But when he saw the wind, he was afraid, and beginning to sink he cried out, 'Lord save me.'"

Peter was doing fine as long as he kept his eyes on Jesus. We have spent a few pages concentrating on ourselves, our strengths, and our weaknesses. We need to do that occasionally, but we always need to get our eyes back on Jesus, our example.

- 1 John 3:1: "See what kind of love the Father has given to us, that we should be called children of God; and so we are."
- 1 John 4:9: "In this the love of God was made manifest among us, that God sent his only Son into the world, so that we might live through him."
- 1 John 4:19: "We love because he first loved us."

Memorize 2 Timothy 1:7. Write it here:

for God has not given us a spirit of timidity, but of power + love + discipline

Who Is Your Friend?

Our goal is to be connected to others as Jesus is to us. How can we be connected to him and be his friend?

"This is my commandment, that you love one another as I have loved you. Greater love has no one than this, that someone lays down his life for his friends. You are my friends if you do what I command you. No longer do I call you servants, for the servant does not know what his master is doing; but I have called you friends, for all that I have heard from my Father I have made known to you. You did not choose me, but I chose you and appointed you that you should go and bear fruit and that your fruit should abide, so that whatever you ask the Father in my name, he may give it to you. These things I command you, so that you will love one another" (John 15:12–17).

As we can see from this passage, loving other people is not a suggestion; it is a command. Our obligation is to love others, wherever they are, however they are, as if they are already our friends.

Unique: 1. Being the only one of its kind: sole. 2. Being without equal or rival.

What Is Your Goal?

🦶 Give others a safe place to be themselves:

> Walk in a manner worthy of the calling to which you have been called, with all humility and gentleness, with patience, bearing with one another in love, eager to maintain the unity of the Spirit in the bond of peace (Ephesians 4:2–3).

🦶 Do not be judgmental. There are no sub-Christians.

> Why do you pass judgment on your brother? Or you, why do you despise your brother? For we will all stand before the judgment seat of God; for it is written, "As I live, says the Lord, every knee shall bow to me, and every tongue shall confess to God." So then each of us will give an account of himself to God. Therefore let us not pass judgment on one another any longer, but rather decide never to put a stumbling block or hindrance in the way of a brother.

. . . So then let us pursue what makes for peace and for mutual upbuilding (Romans 14:10–13, 19).

🎵 Have "the mind of Christ" (1 Corinthians 2:16; Philippians 2:1–16). Having the mind of Christ means loving and serving others "in humility, considering others better than your-selves." Having the mind of Christ means we will love and serve in a way that creates light.

> Therefore if there is any consolation in Christ, if any com-fort of love, if any fellowship of the Spirit, if any affection and mercy, fulfill my joy by being like-minded, having the same love, being of one accord, of one mind. Let nothing be done through selfish ambition or conceit, but in lowliness of mind let each esteem others better than himself. Let each of you look out not only for his own interests, but also for the interests of others.
>
> Let this mind be in you which was also in Christ Jesus, who, being in the form of God, did not consider it robbery to be equal with God, but made himself of no reputation, taking the form of a servant, and coming in the likeness of men. And being found in appearance as a man, he hum-bled himself and became obedient to the point of death, even the death of the cross. Therefore God also has highly exalted him and given him the name which is above every name, that at the name of Jesus every knee should bow, of those in heaven, and of those on earth, and of those under the earth, and that every tongue should confess that Jesus Christ is Lord, to the glory of God the Father.
>
> Therefore, my beloved, as you have always obeyed, not as in my presence only, but now much more in my absence, work out your own salvation with fear and trembling; *for it is God who works in you both to will and to do for his good pleasure.* Do all things without murmuring and disputing, that you may become blameless and harmless, children of God without fault in the midst of a crooked and perverse generation, among whom you shine as lights in the world, holding fast the word of life, so that I may rejoice in the

day of Christ that I have not run in vain or labored in vain. (Philippians 2:1–16 NKJV, emphasis mine).

Be brave: Remember, God works in you "to will and to do." Don't resist. Work with him.

Give me a task too big, too hard for human hands, then I shall come at length to lean on Thee, and leaning, find my strength.

–W. H. Fowler, English Schoolmaster/Lexicographer

Please Hear What I'm Not Saying

Don't be fooled by me.
Don't be fooled by the face I
    wear,
For I wear a mask, a thousand
    masks,
Masks that I'm afraid to take
    off,
And none of them is me.

Pretending is an art that's
    second nature with me,
but don't be fooled,
for God's sake don't be fooled.
I give you the impression that
    I'm secure,
that all is sunny and unruffled
    with me,
within as well as without,
that confidence is my name and
    coolness my game,
that the water's calm and I'm in
    command
and that I need no one,
but don't believe me.

My surface may be smooth, but
my surface is my mask,
ever-varying and
    ever-concealing.
Beneath lies no complacence.
Beneath lies confusion, and fear,
    and aloneness.
But I hide this. I don't want
    anybody to know it.
I panic at the thought of my
    weakness exposed.
That's why I frantically create a
    mask to hide behind,
a nonchalant sophisticated
    façade,
to help me pretend,
to shield me from the glance
    that knows.

But such a glance is precisely
    my salvation,
my only hope, and I know it.
That is, if it is followed by
    acceptance,

73

If it is followed by love.
It's the only thing that can
    liberate me from myself,
from my own self-built prison
    walls,
from the barriers that I so
    painstakingly erect.
It's the only thing that will
    assure me
of what I can't assure myself,
that I'm really worth something.
But I don't tell you this. I don't
    dare to. I'm afraid to.

I'm afraid you'll think less of
    me,
that you'll laugh, and your laugh
    would kill me.
I'm afraid that deep-down I'm
    nothing,
and that you will see this and
    reject me.

So I play my game, my
    desperate, pretending game,
With a façade of assurance
    without
And a trembling child within.
So begins the glittering but
    empty parade of Masks,
And my life becomes a front.
I tell you everything that's
    really nothing,
and nothing of what's
    everything,
of what's crying within me.
So when I'm going through my
    routine,
do not be fooled by what I'm
    saying.

Please listen carefully and try
    to hear what I'm not saying,
what I'd like to be able to say,
what for survival I need to say,
but what I can't say.

I don't like hiding.
I don't like playing superficial
    phony games.
I want to stop playing them.
I want to be genuine and
    spontaneous and me,
but you've got to help me.
You've got to hold out your hand
even when that's the last thing I
    seem to want.
Only you can wipe away from
    my eyes
the blank stare of the breathing
    dead.
Only you can call me into
    aliveness.
Each time you're kind, and
    gentle, and encouraging,
each time you try to understand
    because you really care,
my heart begins to grow
    wings—
very small wings,
but wings!

With your power to touch me
    into feeling,
you can breathe life into me.
I want you to know that.
I want you to know how
    important you are to me,
how you can be a creator—an
    honest-to-God creator—
of the person that is me,
if you choose to.

You alone can break down the
   wall behind which I tremble,
you alone can remove my mask,
you alone can release me from
   the shadow-world of panic,
from my lonely prison,
if you choose to.
Please choose to.

Do not pass me by.
It will not be easy for you.
A long conviction of
   worthlessness builds strong
   walls.
The nearer you approach me,
the blinder I may strike back.
It's irrational, but despite what
   the books may say about
   man,

often I am irrational.
I fight against the very thing I
   cry out for.
But I am told that love is
   stronger than strong walls,
and in this lies my hope.
Please try to beat down those
   walls
with firm hands but with gentle
   hands,
for a child is very sensitive.

Who am I, you may wonder?
I am someone you know very
   well.
For I am every man you meet,
and I am every woman you
   meet.

–Charles C. Finn, ©2011. Used by permission.

Now go out there and give your sisters and brothers a safe place to be themselves. Meet and accept them the way Jesus has accepted you.

Open Your Heart

5

Noon is kind of late to be starting my Saturday chores, but I'm revved up and ready to get it done. It has already been a wonderful morning. Picked up Ms. Jean at 8:30, got her to the hair salon by 9:00, stopped at McD's for breakfast, back to her house by 11:00, chatted a little more, made myself break up the gab-fest, and headed for my house to do my chores by noon.

I don't remember how this routine got started, but I love it. Mostly, I love hearing Ms. Jean's life story: about how she became a Christian and some of her favorite Bible studies; about being a cook in a diner (I see how that experience made her one of the best cooks in the congregation!); listening to the pride in her voice as she talks about her two sons and a daughter—she loves being their mother. She has gotten awfully discouraged since she had to stop driving. She told me this morning with a gleam in her eye that she sometimes drives the five or six blocks to the Dollar Store instead of calling for help.

Ms. Jean is closer to a hundred than she is to ninety, so she must be in the last few steps of her journey. She has been a blessing to the church all of her adult life and even now, when she can barely see and must use a walker to get around in her own house, she is still a blessing. Yes, it's noon, and there's laundry and cleaning and grocery shopping to do, but because of my time with Ms. Jean, "there's within my heart a melody."

> Having purified your souls by your obedience to the truth for a sincere brotherly love, love one another earnestly from a pure heart (1 Peter 1:22).

Christ was God and human at the same time. He had power, and not just any old power. He had the power of God—power to create and power to destroy. But here's an interesting thought: Even as a child, Jesus used this power, not to create or destroy, but to submit to his parents. Throughout his life he used his awesome power to listen to others, care for others, and encourage others. He also used it to heal the sick and encourage those who lived in shame and disgrace. He used his power to glorify God by helping others.

Those characteristics were not limited to his time among men. He was like this before, during, and after his life on earth. And he still has a servant's heart. He lives "to make intercession" for Christians (Hebrews 7:25). He exists to help us.

Jesus did not serve others in order to get them to do what he wanted. He served because it is his nature to serve.

Look again at Peter's response to Jesus when he approached Peter to wash his feet (John 13:3–17). Can't you picture Peter when Jesus knelt before him with a towel and a basin of water? Peter might have been thinking, "Get up! What are you doing? Leaders don't act like that! God's Son does not do dirty work!" Whatever Peter thought, Jesus said, "If I do not wash you, you have no share with me." God is a serving God, and if you reject the serving God, you reject the God who can save you.

In John 14:8, Philip asked Jesus, "Show us the Father." Jesus replied, "Whoever has seen me has seen the Father." What Jesus showed them, and us, is his willingness to put up with verbal abuse and threats. He spent long hours showing others how valuable they are, caring for the sick and needy, and speaking words that give hope and shed light. The disciples equated deity with power and majesty and awesome glory. Deity is all that, and we see it all through the creation story and God's promise-keeping through the Old Testament. But in these same events, we can see God serving his creation. One example is the book of Isaiah, which describes God as a servant.

Our word for this chapter is "sincere," from 1 Peter 1:22. I heard in a sermon many, many years ago that the word is from the Latin *sine* which means "without," and *cera* which means "wax." The speaker went on to say that the word was a pottery term. When the potter slipped up and the clay pot cracked, he might use wax to seal the crack, making it useful again for decorative purposes only, because when the sun melted the wax the pot would fall apart. Shoppers would have to ask, "Is this pot sincere? Is it unbroken?" Searching for confirmation of this story, I found that most etymologies say there is no confirmation of this story, or the story about bricklayers who used wax to repair breaks in a brick and when the sun melted the wax the bricks shifted and houses fell. But the KJV Online Dictionary does define sincere as meaning *without wax* "as if applied originally to pure honey." Whether the stories are true or not, the point is if we are sincere our efforts will be pure and reliable.

Sincere (Greek *anupokritos*) From two words: "a"; not and "hupokrinomai"; hypocrite—without hypocrisy, unfeigned, undisguised 2. True 3. Presenting no false appearance, honest.

Start seeing connections in simple ways and show love sincerely.

Choose Your Adventure

God could push and crush and coerce you into being connected to him. But he doesn't. That's not the way to get someone's heart, and your heart is what he wants. When you long to be connected to someone, isn't it your hearts you want connected?

Start seeing connections in simple ways. It is time to open the gate in your fence and open your heart. Get your heart where it needs to be and your actions will follow.

Here are your options for the week:

1. Greet and welcome a visitor. Invite her to sit with you and your family or friends. Make a note of her name, and be sure to use her name.

2. Sit in a new place each week for Bible study and worship. Make an effort to get better acquainted with someone you may have worshiped with for years but don't know well.

3. Find a member of your congregation who does not often attend a fellowship event. The elders or a friend might help guide you in your search. Ask that person to sit with you and your family. Offer to save a place for him at your table. Tell her you want to get better acquainted.

4. If you rarely or never attend fellowship gatherings because of insecurities or anxieties, find someone to "join up with" before the event. You might offer her a ride so you will have someone with whom to enter the room.

5. Pray for someone who has been missing in attendance. When your heart is full of love for that person, call and tell him that he is missed. That's all. No sermons. You don't need to worry about what to say. Just let him know that he belongs.

Before You Take Action

- 🎵 Read and think about each option.

- 🎵 Make one or more selections from the five options above. Circle your choice/s now.

- 🎵 Why did you select that option?

Circle the appropriate answers about your choice:

- 🎵 I am allowing this assignment to motivate me to remove a barrier that has needed to come down for a long time.

- 🎵 I have decided this is the day to stop passing people by with just a nod and a "hello."

- 🎵 I am comfortable doing any of these things.

- 🎵 Other: _____

Select or supply the reason you did not select the other option(s).

- 🎵 It's too hard.

- 🎵 It's too painful.

- 🎵 It's too _____

- 🎵 Other: _____

Pray and complete the task(s); then answer these questions:

1. How did you feel as you prepared to do the assignment? Afraid of rejection? Afraid of a lack of patience? Confident? Eager? Other: _____.

2. What did you feel when you were with the other person? Kind? Impatient? Intolerant? Strong? Other: _____
_____.

3. Did you listen to them? Why or why not?

4. Describe what you learned about the recipient that helps you understand (a) her perspective, (b) who she is, or (c) what she values.

5. What did you do to show that you valued her?

6. Did your time together go well? Did both of you interact or were your efforts unidirectional? Why did your attempt go as it did?

7. If you both interacted, how does this experience help you connect? Was there a response that might indicate a need has been met? If so, describe the response here and include your thoughts about how your understanding of others has increased.

8. Was there an indication that the recipient feels supported or encouraged? Do you feel encouraged? Why do you feel the way you do?

9. Did the other person or couple reach out to you in return? If so, describe the result.

10. If you are feeling more patient, more tolerant, more under-standing, why do you think that is? Sometimes we don't know what we think until we try to put our thoughts into words. Write your thoughts here:

11. Share your thoughts in class or with a friend who will keep your confidences.

12. Talk to God about the recipient's reaction and your feelings. Give it to God, and let it go. Allow him to work for both of you. How will this communication strengthen you?

Beating Hearts Are Active

I visited a congregation on a Wednesday night. I came in through a side door and began looking for a classroom directory. A couple entering behind me got my attention: "We don't know you. Are you new here?" I told them it was my first visit and that I was looking for an appropriate classroom. When we introduced ourselves, I was delighted to know I was speaking with Stan and Nell, and that Stan was an elder in that congregation. So Nell told me it was singing night and almost everyone would be in the auditorium. After learning I was a soprano, she introduced me to three women who made a place for me on their pew. She welcomed me again and invited me to come again.

The three women asked me about myself and told me a bit about themselves. After the songfest these women, and others sitting around us, invited me to come again. We chatted for about twenty minutes. No one seemed to be in a hurry to get away from me and back to their own lives.

My next visit was on Sunday morning. As I entered the auditorium, at least five people stopped me and introduced themselves. One woman took me by the arm and invited me to sit with her. On each of my first half dozen visits, someone different offered me a seat. One gave me her phone number and invited me to call her during the week.

There is no way a person can feel invisible with that kind of attention. Attendance there runs just under five hundred. I have worshiped in many loving, supportive congregations but have never had so many who made me feel significant just because I exist. They didn't wait to find out if I was important or useful before they treated me so. I was important simply because I was there.

The way those Christians behaved had nothing to do with me. It was about Christ living in them and their service to God. How can you not want to be with people like that all the time? How can you not want to be loving and giving in return? *This* is why we are spending time thinking about how to draw others in. We want all to find a place and purpose in the body of Christ.

Personal Reflections

6

Stretch Out Your Hands

Enrolling at Freed-Hardeman College, about three hundred miles from home, provided me my first opportunity to experience the church without my mother. "Thank you, God, for letting this happen at the Estes Church of Christ." I traveled there from campus on a bus with students I didn't know to a church building full of brothers and sisters I didn't know. Brothers and sisters, that's how we used to greet each other: brother Scott, sister Hibbett. I could have become invisible, but the members at Estes wouldn't let me. They made eye contact. They learned my name and something about me. They invited small groups of students into their homes where we could get to know each other. I was in the group that went to sister Jackie Hibbett's house. I distinctly remember the singing, talking, and laughing as we enjoyed dinner around a big table, cleared the table, and then moved into a large room where we had a devotional and became acquainted with one another.

At some point I felt tears well up in my eyes. Oh horrors, I rushed to the bathroom where I could express my feelings without embarrassing anyone. Sister Hibbett and sister Tucker came and soothed me and reassured me it was just homesickness and that was a good thing. Homesickness means you have a good home and you miss it. I was homesick, but it was not homesickness that made me cry. I cried because I was seeing clearly and personally what the church is supposed to be like.

When you have always worshiped with your mama and the friends with whom you have grown up, that is the norm for your life. But when you are suddenly a stranger among many Christians, you begin to see things you never have noticed before, things you have taken for granted. What I saw those first weeks at Estes, and specifically in the home of the Hibbetts, was adults, strangers, busy people taking time to help me find my place. At assembly, one of the elders, brother Tom Scott, always greeted me by name and asked about my classes or my week or something, anything that made me feel he really cared that I was in attendance. The message I received loud and clear at Estes was "Your place is right here, right here with us." I was neither invisible to this congregation nor insignificant. That is the way it is supposed to be in the church. I learned it at Estes, and I learned it for my life.

Work with your hands, as we instructed you, so that you may live properly before outsiders and be dependent on no one (1 Thessalonians 4:11–12).

Whatever your hand finds to do, do it with your might (Ecclesiastes 9:10).

As each has received a gift, use it to serve one another, as good stewards of God's varied grace: whoever speaks, as one who speaks oracles of God; whoever serves, as one who serves by the strength that God supplies—in order that in everything God may be glorified through Jesus Christ. To him belong glory and dominion forever and ever. Amen (1 Peter 4:10–11).

STRETCH OUT YOUR HANDS

STRETCH OUT YOUR HANDS

Some Christians would have us believe that to be considered faithful we must knock on doors and teach home Bible studies. Clearly, Peter wants us to know that we also teach by serving. We are to use the gift God gave us—whatever it is—to glorify him. The woman who takes homegrown tomatoes to a neighbor in the name of Jesus glorifies God. When she takes stock of what she can do and does it, she is valuable to the body. Sometimes we mistakenly think that only those who teach Bible classes glorify the Father. But the Christian who gives someone a ride, mows a yard, or babysits in the name of Jesus so a weary mother can catch a nap, glorifies God.

Using your hands to distribute relief and receiving recognition can provide you with an opportunity to say, "No. No. You don't owe me anything. God has blessed me, and I am sharing." Anything you do that points someone toward God or draws that person closer to the Lord glorifies God. Open your hands to serve.

Jesus used his hands to connect with others. He touched a leper (Matthew 8:1–3), gave sight to the blind (Matthew 9:29–30; 20:29–34), healed Peter's mother-in-law (Matthew 8:15), raised a ruler's daughter (Matthew 9:25), made the deaf hear (Mark 7:33–35), and blessed little children (Mark 10:13–16). Jesus touched his disciples (Matthew 17:7), and his disciples touched him (1 John 1:1). He also allowed others to touch him, for instance, the sick in the marketplace (Mark 6:56) and the sinful woman who anointed Jesus' feet with her tears and dried them with her hair (Luke 7:36–38).

Notice the value of Jesus' touch:

> When he came down from the mountain, great crowds followed him. And behold, a leper came to him and knelt before him, saying, "Lord, if you will, you can make me clean." And Jesus stretched out his hand and touched him, saying, "I will; be clean." And immediately his leprosy was cleansed (Matthew 8:1–3).

89

Jesus had healed others just by speaking, so we know he could have healed this leper just by speaking. But he didn't; he touched him. Perhaps we don't appreciate the depth of this healing because we don't understand the horror of leprosy in the first century. Perhaps it will help to compare it to AIDS in the '70s and '80s.

We were, and still are, afraid of AIDS. In the 1970s we didn't want to be in the same room with AIDS patients. Some didn't want to be in the same community with them. We definitely didn't want to touch them. That's how it was for lepers in the first century. For the Jews it was not only dangerous to touch a leper, but it was also forbidden by God.

Glorify (Greek *doxazo*): To praise, extol, magnify, celebrate, or honor. Make glorious. To cause the dignity and worth of some person or thing to become manifest and acknowledged.

Lepers had to leave mainstream society and live "outside the camp," alone or with other lepers. If someone touched a leper, he was deemed unclean and had to go through a purification process. And yet, a leper dared to approach Jesus for healing. The words, "be healed," coming from Jesus' lips would have been sufficient. Instead, Jesus stretched out his hand and touched him. He touched him! What a beautiful picture of compassion. Jesus understood the generous gift of touching someone ostracized by society, touching someone who has not felt the warmth and caring touch of another human for some time.

Choose Your Adventure

Remember to pray before you choose an assignment, and then select your method of approach. You may choose to do something that isn't listed. The goal is to focus on the other person and on what occurs when you try to connect.

As you work your way through your task(s), see how serving with your hands initiates connections. Here are three suggestions:

1. *Choose a widow in the congregation.* Take her a meal or a dish of food. Eat with her if you can make the time. People who live alone often find it difficult to eat alone.

2. *Choose a senior single or couple.* Do something for them that would be physically difficult, such as changing ceiling light bulbs, cleaning up high or down low, moving something manageable for you but difficult or impossible for the elderly.

3. *Choose a single person who does not have family nearby and give her hugs and contact.* Touch is healing. Give hugs or handshakes or pats on the shoulder. Couple that appropriate touch with direct eye contact.

Before You Take Action

- Read and think about each option.
- Make a selection. You may choose one or more of the suggested options or create one of your own.
- Think about why you selected that option.

Circle the appropriate answers about your choice

- I am comfortable with (older people, young people, couples).
- I am not comfortable with (older people, young people, couples). I wish to become more comfortable with that group.
- I won't have to travel far; someone lives near me.
- I am a pretty good cook.
- It is easy for me to start a conversation with, "Hi. I brought you this."

🎵 I live alone and understand the situation.

🎵 I know someone who will appreciate it.

🎵 I know someone who has a need that is not being met.

🎵 I have family members in similar situations, so I understand and empathize.

🎵 I am "handy."

🎵 I am not a hugger, but I want to become one.

🎵 I am comfortable doing any of these things.

🎵 Other_____

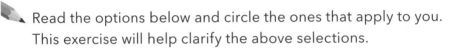 Read the options below and circle the ones that apply to you. This exercise will help clarify the above selections.

🎵 I am not comfortable with (older people, young people, couples).

🎵 I am not a toucher.

🎵 I don't have time.

🎵 Other _____

Pay Attention! Don't Just Go through the Motions.

Using your hands to reach out to people can put you beside them but not connected. What makes a connection? You must understand each other to some degree.

Often we do things for people without paying attention to their response. Our reaching out might make us feel good but make them feel terrible. This book is not only about the doing. It's about being and seeing and understanding. Spend some time in silence thinking about your efforts and their effects.

Pray and complete your task(s). Then answer these questions:

1. How did you feel as you prepared to do the assignment? Afraid of rejection; silly; brave; other _____.

2. What did you feel when you were with the other person/couple? Nervous; happy; afraid; or _____.

3. Did you listen to them? If not, make a commitment to do more listening from now on. Write your promise here:

4. Describe what you learned about the recipient that helps you understand (a) their perspective, (b) who they are, and (c) what they value.

5. What did you do to show them you value them?

6. If there was no response from the person with whom you chose to interact, what do you think that means?

7. If there was a response, describe it here:

8. Was there a response that might indicate that a need was met? If so, describe your reasoning here:

9. Was there an indication that healing occurred? If so, describe it here:

10. Was there an indication that the recipient felt supported or encouraged? What makes you think so?

11. What did you learn that will help you in the future?

12. Did the other person or couple reach out to you in return? If so, describe that here:

13. Was your bucket filled? Was her bucket filled? What makes you think so?

Share, Don't Gossip

Connecting might be easy for you. You might be comfortable with all the assignment choices. If so, wonderful! Thank you for participating—outside and inside of class. Discussing or sharing your thoughts in class might help others understand their experiences.

Share with the class how your contact responded, but do not gossip. There is no need to share her name or personal details. Share your perspective. Share what you learned about yourself.

For example: "The session with my contact went (well, not so well). I felt (relaxed, awkward). The other person seemed (at ease, suspicious, puzzled)."

Or maybe on a strictly positive level you could say, "It was fun! I found out we have things in common." Or, "I was able to provide some information about a resource she needed. I was there at just the right time."

Talk to God about the recipient's reaction and your feelings. Give it to God, and let it go. Allow him to work for both of you.

You may trust the Lord too little, but
you can never trust him too much.
–Unknown

Open Your Mouth

7

> Therefore encourage one another and build one another up, just as you are doing (1 Thessalonians 5:11).

Maybe you never meet a stranger, or maybe you freeze in social climates. Either way, you will benefit from the information and experience to be gained from this chapter.

It is time to speak up. But before you open your mouth, let's examine a few basic facts about communication. According to John Powell in his book, *Why Am I Afraid to Tell You Who I Am?* there are five levels of communication ranking from the bottom of the pyramid to the top, from basic conversation to intimate conversation.

Peak Communication

My Feelings (Gut Level)

My Ideas and Judgments

Reporting the Facts about Others

Cliché Conversation

Cliché Conversation

Generally, when we first meet someone socially, our conversations consist of clichés like: "How are you?" "I like your dress." "It's good to see you." "How 'bout those Yankees?" "It sure is hot, isn't it?" There is nothing threatening or intrusive in these comments. (Well, except, perhaps the one about the Yankees.) Everyone remains safe—and unconnected. However, this level of communication can be used to initiate connection. When you ask, "How are you?" wait for the answer. Make eye contact. When you say, "I like your dress," be genuine. Make eye contact. I know I just said that, but it cannot be said too often or done too often. Eye contact implies some level of acceptance. Connection doesn't occur without accepting the other person.

Communicate: 1. To have an interchange as of ideas or information. 2. To express oneself effectively.

At this level of communication, you might find that just calling the other person by name will initiate a connection. When I was a missionary in South Africa a lifetime ago, I prepared myself and my children for culture shock by deciding to adopt the cultural differences that would allow me to not only be myself but a better person. One of the first things I noticed was that in conversation, South Africans call people by their names often. They have a saying, "*She* is the cat's mother." Parents used this phrase to teach children to use fewer pronouns and call people by their names. I heard my name more times in the first few weeks of our six years there than I had heard it in all my life before. I never felt invisible in South Africa. School teachers have told me that simply calling a student's name will often restore order. Movies sometime depict the mob being broken up when others begin to use the real names of the miscreants. When a person is named, he knows he is visible, recognized as a whole and separate person.

Four-year-old Billy said it this way, "When someone loves you, the way they say your name is different. You know that your name is safe in their mouth."

Reporting Facts

When you share generally known facts, you reveal almost nothing about yourself and invite nothing from others. You just pass information along. "The next ballgame is on Monday," or "You are on chapter 5."

You can stop at this level, but if you do, you are failing to connect. You remain only adjacent. How do you begin with fact-reporting and move onward? After you deliver information to her, such as "Monday Night for the Master is tomorrow at seven," invite her to attend. Offer her a ride or tell her, "I will wait for you at the front door," or "I'll save you a seat at my table." Do what you can to make her feel wanted and included.

Sharing Ideas and Judgments

Do you have trouble trusting others? Most of us test the waters when we begin to share our ideas and judgments. If the other person raises her eyebrows or narrows her eyes or if she yawns or looks at her watch, we might retreat to safer ground by being silent or changing the subject. But if she remains interested and shares something about herself in return, trust starts to develop and bonding begins.

Webster's Dictionary defines *judgment* as "the ability to make decisions or form opinions by discerning and evaluating." The definition of *discern* is "to perceive (something hidden or obscure); to perceive differences."

Sharing Feelings

When I trust you, I can begin to share feelings that lie under my ideas and those judgments and convictions that are uniquely mine. By judgment I mean things like, "I think our president is doing a good/bad job," and by feelings, I mean things like "I am jealous" or "I am proud to be your friend" or "I feel ill at ease when _____."

Peak Communication

Sometimes we have difficulty connecting because we think most people don't want to hear our gut feelings, so we dissemble and settle for superficial relationships. However, with those who have proven to be trustworthy, we should take the risk in sharing ourselves. We might then begin to see how alike we are, or we might find that our differences are complementary. If that happens, we have the potential of sharing peak communication, which is not a permanent experience but occurs in moments of mutual empathy. Treasured moments, aren't they?

In a comment on Pinterest, Victoria Erickson said,

> When connections are real, they simply never die. They can be buried or ignored or walked away from, but never broken. If you've deeply resonated with another person or place, the connection remains despite any distance, time, situation, lack of presence, or circumstance. If you're doubtful then just try it. Revisit a person or place and see if there's any sense at all of the space between now and then. If it was truly real, you'll be instantly swept back into the moment it was before it left—during the same year and place with the same wonder and hope, comfort and heartbeat. Real connections live on forever.

Learn to Encourage

♪ *Be like Barnabas.* "Anybody can sympathize with the sufferings of a friend, but it requires a very fine nature to sympathize with a friend's success" (Oscar Wilde).

> The report of this came to the ears of the church in Jerusalem, and they sent Barnabas to Antioch. When he came and saw the grace of God, he was glad [because that was the kind of man he was], and he exhorted them all to remain faithful to the Lord with steadfast purpose, for he was a good man, full of the Holy Spirit and of faith. And a great many people were added to the Lord (Acts 11:22–24, brackets mine).

Give another example of Barnabas' encouragement.

From Ecclesiastes 3:1–8, list at least three times of life when encouragement is needed.

♪ *Don't be a busybody.* "Besides that, they learn to be idlers, going about from house to house, and not only idlers, but also gossips and busybodies, saying what they should not" (1 Timothy 5:13).

♪ *Do make right judgments.* "Do not judge by appearances, but judge with right judgment" (John 7:24). Another excellent example of how to make right judgments is found earlier in John 7 when Jesus spoke plainly to the Jews about their failure to obey the law, to which the crowd answered, "You have a demon!" (John 7:20). Jesus responded with a simple and logical explanation. Don't base judgments on gut feelings or appearances but on evidence and facts.

Choose Your Adventure

Think about the levels of communication needed as you use your voice to connect with others in one of the following suggestions. Consider how to increase the connection by using a higher level of communication, by being genuine. Wait for the answer to your cliché question and draw the other person out, calling her by name.

1. Call someone in the congregation just to say "good job," "glad to know you," "thank you," or "I'm sorry (for your loss, that you are ill, whatever)."

2. Visit someone who is homebound, in the hospital, or in a nursing home. That task might seem difficult at first, but all you need to do is show up. That in itself is a gift. You might ask, "Are you having a good day?" Give your hostess an opportunity to talk if she wishes. The visit is about her, not you. Don't stay too long; she needs rest. An appropriate touch might be a pat or touch on the shoulder. Touch is healing. It is always a good idea to ask if the person wants to pray with you. But if either of you is uncomfortable with that, tell her you will pray for her at home.

3. Choose a person you have been acquainted with for years, perhaps, but the relationship has not developed deeply. Have a conversation that moves beyond cliché and reporting facts by sharing your ideas, feelings and/or judgments on a subject. (Examples: "What do you think about the areas of service offered by our congregation?" "How is our Wednesday night Bible class helping you to understand God's relationship with the Israelites in the wilderness?")

4. Organize a group to sing at a nursing home, or join a group that is already organized. God gives us a song: "He put a new song in my mouth, a song of praise to our God" (Psalm 40:3). "The Lord is my strength and my song; he has become my salvation" (Psalm 118:14).

5. Discuss a personal fear with a trustworthy friend. Vividly describe it.

Before You Take Action

- Read and think about each option from the previous five suggestions.
- Make a selection, choosing one or more options. Circle your choice now.
- Think about why you selected that option. Make a note of your reasoning here:

Circle the appropriate answers about your choice:

- I enjoy patting other people on the back.
- I take pleasure in making other people feel better.
- Meeting new people is an adventure for me.
- I like to organize groups.
- It is easy for me to include others in service events.
- I am comfortable doing any of these things.
- Other _____

Circle why you did not select another option.

- ♪ I'm not comfortable giving praise to others.
- ♪ It's embarrassing to praise others.
- ♪ I feel pretentious when I praise others.
- ♪ I have no friend with whom I dare trust my fears.
- ♪ Other _____

Pray and complete the task(s); then answer these questions:

1. How did you feel as you prepared to do the assignment? Afraid of rejection? Silly? Brave? Other?

2. What did you feel when you were with the other person/couple? Nervous? Happy? Afraid? Other?

3. Did you listen to them? Do you remember what they said? Briefly relate what you heard here:

4. Describe what you learned about the recipient that helps you understand (a) their perspective, or (b) who they are, or (c) what they value.

5. What did you do to show them you value them?

6. If there was no response from the one approached, what do you think that means?

7. If there was a response, describe it here:

8. Was there a response that might indicate a need has been met? If so, describe the response here:

9. Was there an indication that healing occurred? If so, describe it here:

10. Was there an indication that the recipient felt supported or encouraged?

11. Did the other person reach out to you in return? If so, describe that here:

12. Using the chart at the beginning of this chapter, indicate the level of communication that occurred in this assignment. The purpose of this question is not to make a judgment, but to provide an additional opportunity to consider the different levels of communication.

13. Comment here about any response or lack of response to your frequent use of someone's name.

If you are comfortable, share your thoughts in class or with a trustworthy friend. Talk to God about everything you discovered or relearned in this chapter. Give it to God, and let it go. Allow him to work for both you and the ones with whom you are trying to connect.

Share Kind Deeds

8

Elise snapped the clasp on her bracelet and gave a final pat to her hair. There. All set to go. "Lucy. Ready?" "Almost, Mom!" shouted her daughter. Unsurprised, Elise sat down on the sofa with her husband who was patiently waiting while reading the newspaper. Elise smiled as she thought about the festivities to come: a teacher appreciation dinner at the church building. This would be the fourth one for her. She had been teaching for seventeen years and the dinner was held every five years. She always enjoyed them. But she didn't need to be thanked because she loved teaching the four-year-olds. They soaked up Bible stories the way a dry sponge soaks up water. Teaching them was the talent God had given her, so every year she attended teacher training workshops to improve her skills, get new ideas, and get inspired. Seventeen years, and she still loved it. Still, it was nice of the congregation to recognize teachers' efforts.

Elise's thoughts wandered to her classroom, an inviting and cheerful place. Parents told her their children were eager for Bible class on Sunday morning. This quarter, Anna, her co-teacher, had decorated one bulletin board with the children's favorite character, Little Bear, and the other board with a mother duck, baby ducklings, butterflies, and a pond with a frog on a lily pad. That Anna! Every quarter new bulletin boards that coordinated with the curriculum appeared like magic. Elise knew that as a wife and mother who also worked outside the home, she just didn't have time to prepare the lessons and create the bulletin boards. "Thank you, God, for Anna!"

In the previous chapter, we looked at how we use oral communication to initiate and deepen connection. In this chapter let's consider how our actions can do the same. In 1 John 3:18, the apostle John pleads with us to love each other in deed (with actions) and in truth. Kind deeds are part of the foundation to our bonding.

 How have kind deeds contributed to one solid relationship in your experience?

In the "Elise and Anna" example at the beginning of the chapter, who was receiving public recognition? How important were Anna's kind deeds?

 Expressing Love

At the 2013 Freed-Hardeman Bible Lectures, Rosemary McKnight applied Gary Chapman's book, *The Five Love Languages,* to the church community. He suggests there are five

languages whereby each of us expresses love and feels loved
in return: (1) words of affirmation, (2) quality time (3) giving
and receiving gifts, (4) acts of service, and (5) physical touch.
Whether or not you are familiar with this book, it is well worth
the investment.

As you seek to make connections, spend some time watching
people. Observe their behavior and try to determine how they
express love. Such expressions are often an indication of the
kinds of behaviors that make them feel loved.

Words of Affirmation

According to Rosemary McKnight, people who send cards—
thank you, get well, birthday—are trying to connect using words
of affirmation. They are using this method of communication
to tell others they are loved. They will pat you on the back and
say, "Good job." In general conversation, they tell you that you
look nice or they like your tie. They will thank the teacher for
her time and preparation. Chances are, people will recognize
that you love them if you use this method to express your love to
them. Don't we all need at least an occasional good word from
others? Words of commendation are encouraging and definitely
fit the description for kind deeds.

> Let your speech always be gracious, seasoned with salt, so that
> you may know how you ought to answer each person (Colossians 4:6).

> The tongue of the righteous is choice silver; the heart of the
> wicked is of little worth. The lips of the righteous feed many,
> but fools die for lack of sense (Proverbs 10:20–21).

> Anxiety in a man's heart weighs him down, but a good word
> makes him glad (Proverbs 12:25).

While we are talking about words of affirmation, make sure you say words of affirmation to yourself. Instead of "I am so stupid," perhaps you could say, "Well, that was not the smartest thing I've done. Next time I will . . ." Every cell in your body hears the words you speak to yourself. Nourish yourself.

 Consider the statement "I can do all things through him who strengthens me" (Philippians 4:13). How does the Bible provide personal affirmation? Find two additional affirmations in the Psalms.

Quality Time

Do you see people expressing love by visiting the sick and shut-ins at home or in a nursing home? They are giving of their pre-cious time. Because they see spending time with someone as a way to express love,

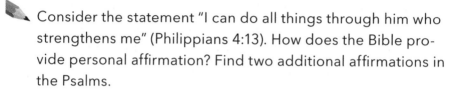

Observe: 1. To notice; perceive. 2. To watch attentively.

they are very appreciative when you take the time to ask them to sit with you at fellowship time or when you move to where they are in order to find out how life is going for them. According to my dear sister, Sherry James, "Quality time is purposeful rather than accidental time spent together."

> And let us consider how to stir up one another to love and good works, not neglecting to meet together, as is the habit of some, but encouraging one another, and all the more as you see the Day drawing near (Hebrews 10:24–25).

Fill in the blanks:

"Two are better than one, because they have a good _____ for their toil. For if they fall, one will _____ up his fellow. But woe to him who is _____ when he falls and has not another to lift him up! Again, if two lie together, they keep warm, but how can one keep warm _____? And though a man might prevail against one who is alone, two will withstand him—a threefold cord is not quickly _____ " (Ecclesiastes 4:9–12).

How do two people have a threefold cord?

If your answer to this question was "by including God," I like it and agree with you. Also, it's a thing called *synergy*. This word was coined in the '70s to describe what happens when two people work on a project and complete it in one-third the time it would take a single person. One person has energy, two have synergy. God didn't inspire Solomon to use the word *synergy*, but he did inspire him to describe it.

Giving and Receiving Gifts

People who express love through kind deeds such as giving gifts are those you see giving homemade bread, bringing a small item they saw in their travels that reminded them of you, or bringing a flower or plant from their gardens. For these people, even a gift from a bubblegum machine means a lot, because it means you thought of them at a time when you weren't together.

> Give, and it will be given to you. Good measure, pressed down, shaken together, running over, will be put into your lap. For with the measure you use it will be measured back to you (Luke 6:38).

Reflect on the events of the past month. What "measure" are you expecting based on your giving?

> In all things I have shown you that by working hard in this way we must help the weak and remember the words of the Lord Jesus, how he himself said, "It is more blessed to give than to receive" (Acts 20:35).

 How will you encourage "the weak" this week?

 Write John 3:16 in the space below and circle the giver, the gift, and the ultimate reward. Then find two more examples from scripture that motivate you in giving.

Acts of Service

Those who give and receive love through kind deeds are preparing meals for the sick and bereaved, babysitting, driving someone to and from church services or to the doctor's office, and perhaps teaching Bible classes. These people get frustrated when people offer to help and then don't show up. They feel burdened when it seems to them they are the only ones working.

For you were called to freedom, brothers. Only do not use your freedom as an opportunity for the flesh, but through love serve one another (Galatians 5:13).

So then, as we have opportunity, let us do good to everyone, and especially to those who are of the household of faith (Galatians 6:10).

Why is it difficult to serve in a volunteer army?

What would happen in a secular job if a person failed to show up as agreed?

How is failure to keep your word a form of lying?

Be a light! It is important to let your light shine, to let it be known that you are working in your part of the vineyard. I'm not talking about tooting your horn. There is a difference between letting your light shine and shining your light. If your light is on, people will see it without your shining it, and that's a good thing.

Fill in the blanks

"Let another praise you, and not your _____ _____" (Proverbs 27:2).

"Sound no trumpet before you . . . that [you] may be _____ by others" (Matthew 6:2).

Plan to have a conversation this week with a person whose light is shining brightly. Ask specifically about her personal time in God's word. How do you perceive her links with others?

You are being asked every week to tell your class what happened when you completed certain tasks. Have you noticed that the questions are about what you are learning? None of us are born knowing everything. We learn by watching others, listening as others describe their successes and failures, and reading about methods. We also learn from our own efforts, including mistakes, if we are wise. Sharing your experience in class makes you an example. I know I keep saying this, but I want you to be convinced that orally sharing what you have learned is a blessing to you and to those who hear you.

"Show yourself in all respects to be a model of good works, and in your teaching show integrity, dignity" (Titus 2:7). How does this verse relate to "Acts of Service"?

Comment on the phrase "in all respects" from Titus 2:7.

Your experiences are important to others. Don't hesitate to share them in class. You are an adult. You can figure out how to tell others of your successes and failures with integrity and dignity, without sounding a trumpet or with false modesty. Your experiences are significant.

> For who sees anything different in you? What do you have that you did not receive? If then you received it, why do you boast as if you did not receive it? (1 Corinthians 4:7).

If a woman has a great talent, how can she give God the glory for her gift?

If a woman has a small talent, how can she give God the glory for her gift?

When we realize we can't take all the credit for what we know and for how well we do things, it's harder to boast. If I know something, I learned it the hard way or someone shared it with me. I have nothing to brag about and neither do you. We are all just trying to please God as best we can.

Physical Touch

I am very thankful for people who know what appropriate touch is and are not afraid to do so. I'm not just talking about those who greet another with a hug or a handshake. I'm also talking about those who rock the babies in the nursery so mothers and dads can hear the whole sermon. I'm talking about those who hold hands and pray together. And don't forget shoulder bumps and fist bumps. They count as appropriate touch. But here is a caution for those who feel they must touch in order to show love. Learn what it means to touch appropriately. Some do not like to be touched except by those closest to them. One of my daughters-in-law is not the touchy-feely type. But she knows I love and need hugs, at least occasionally, so she makes sure she gives me a hug when we greet each other and say goodbye. It is one of the most precious gifts she gives me, because I know what it costs her and because I know she does it for me.

Jesus didn't touch only the beautiful. He touched those whom no one else would touch:

> And behold, a leper came to him and knelt before him, saying, "Lord, if you will, you can make me clean." And Jesus stretched out his hand and touched him, saying, "I will; be clean." And immediately his leprosy was cleansed (Matthew 8:2–3).

> And when Jesus entered Peter's house, he saw his mother-in-law lying sick with a fever. He touched her hand, and the fever left her, and she rose and began to serve him (Matthew 8:14–15).

Outdo in Showing Honor

These few paragraphs have barely touched on the message of Gary Chapman's book. Rosemary McKnight helped me understand how to apply the message of the book in my congregation. This little book is also helpful in connecting with our physical families. For instance, do you express love by cooking? Most mothers do, but consider this. Perhaps a daughter, especially one who is watching her weight, might feel more loved if you cooked less and listened more? To be connected deeply, we must show love—not only in the ways we value but also in the ways that have meaning to others.

For as in one body we have many members, and the members do not all have the same function, so we, though many, are one body in Christ, and individually members one of another. Having gifts that differ according to the grace given to us, let us use them . . . Let love be genuine . . . Outdo one another in showing honor (Romans 12:4–6, 9–10).

Each person is uniquely designed by God. Respect the differences. You were born an original. Don't die a copy, and don't try to make everyone else think and do and be just like you. Try to meet people where they are.

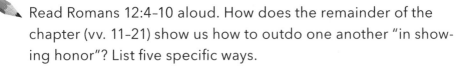

Read Romans 12:4-10 aloud. How does the remainder of the chapter (vv. 11-21) show us how to outdo one another "in showing honor"? List five specific ways.

Choose Your Adventure

Before you choose this week's assignment, spend some time deciphering love languages based on the behavior of others. Then show your love, genuinely, in a way that is recognizable to the person with whom you want to connect. Remember, the suggestions in this section are simply that: suggestions. If you find a better way to connect, use it. As you work your plan, think about Gary Chapman's love languages. Connections occur when we understand another person.

These tasks are not about you. These suggestions are not for making someone else become as you are. They are opportunities for you to get to know others and get to know yourself. They open the door. If you are attentive to what you see beyond the door, you will learn about yourself and about the other person. You just might move beyond cliché to a higher level of fellowship—if you are paying attention.

1. Take an inexpensive or homemade gift to someone who enjoys giving similar gifts to others: a pie, a plant, a potholder, a small remembrance that has your love as a wrapping.

2. Invite someone who enjoys visiting the sick and shut-ins to sit with you in worship, join you at your table, or join you and your friends in conversation.

3. Send a "Just Because" card to someone who enjoys encouraging others.

4. Do a good deed by helping a Bible class teacher with making visual aids.

5. Volunteer to transfer food from someone who is preparing food for a grieving family.

6. Make it a practice to touch huggers appropriately. Even if you are not a hugger, you could bump a friend's shoulder, pat someone on the back or arm, touch another's elbow, or shake a stranger's hand.

 Before You Take Action

 Read and think about each option.

Decide which ones you want to try.

Think about why you selected that option.

Why did you so choose? Why did you not make a different selection?

After you prayerfully complete your assignment, answer the questions below. You might be getting tired of the repetitiveness of these questions, but please proceed patiently. Remember that the goal of this study is to learn to connect with people by being in the moment. The questions are to help you focus on the experience and recall it. Being able to answer the questions will help you synthesize, that is, to recall and retell in order to create new meaning or understanding. Synthesizing enables you to apply new understanding to other tasks.

So as Mr. Miyagi told Daniel-san in *The Karate Kid:* "Focus," and "Wax on. Wax off." We improve our skills through practice.

As you tried to initiate or deepen connections this week, how did you apply the "Five Love Languages" we studied? Relate your thoughts here.

1. Describe an observed behavior that allowed you to apply one of the love languages.

2. How did your understanding of the love languages help you to show others that you value them?

3. Describe the responses that indicated a need has been met.

4. Why do you believe the recipient felt, or did not feel, supported or encouraged?

5. If your target person responded to your approach, describe that response.

6. Share your thoughts with the class or with a trustworthy friend.

Talk to God about the recipient's reaction and your feelings. Give it to God, and let it go. Allow him to work for both of you.

9

Meditate and Evaluate

Finally, brothers, whatever is true, whatever is honorable, whatever is just, whatever is pure, whatever is lovely, whatever is commendable, if there is any excellence, if there is anything worthy of praise, think about these things (Philippians 4:8).

God blesses everyone. Those the Lord will separate to his right hand are those who receive God's blessings and give food, drink, shelter, clothes, and time. Those who will be separated to the Lord's left hand are those who selfishly accept God's blessings and give little-to-nothing to others.

"When the Son of Man comes in his glory, and all the angels with him, then he will sit on his glorious throne. Before him will be gathered all the nations, and he will separate people one from another as a shepherd separates the sheep from the goats. And he will place the sheep on his right, but the goats on the left. Then the King will say to those on his right, 'Come, you who are blessed by my Father, inherit the kingdom prepared for you from the foundation of the world. For I was hungry and you gave me food, I was thirsty and you gave me drink, I was a stranger and you welcomed me, I was naked and you clothed me, I was sick and you visited me, I was in prison and you came to me.' Then the righteous will answer him, saying, 'Lord, when did we see

121

you hungry and feed you, or thirsty and give you drink? And when did we see you a stranger and welcome you, or naked and clothe you? And when did we see you sick or in prison and visit you?' And the King will answer them, 'Truly, I say to you, as you did it to one of the least of these my brothers, you did it to me.'

"Then he will say to those on his left, 'Depart from me, you cursed, into the eternal fire prepared for the devil and his angels. For I was hungry and you gave me no food, I was thirsty and you gave me no drink, I was a stranger and you did not welcome me, naked and you did not clothe me, sick and in prison and you did not visit me.' Then they also will answer, saying, 'Lord, when did we see you hungry or thirsty or a stranger or naked or sick or in prison, and did not minister to you?' Then he will answer them, saying, 'Truly, I say to you, as you did not do it to one of the least of these, you did not do it to me.' And these will go away into eternal punishment, but the righteous into eternal life" (Matthew 25:31–46).

According to this passage, there are two kinds of people: givers and takers.

Be a Giver

In order to create ties that bind us together, we must give. Our greatest gift is time: time to consider and plan, time to execute, and time to think about what works and what doesn't work.

We should continue to remember that God wants the members of the body to be linked to each other and to him. However, Satan does not want that to happen. He is happy when we are disconnected, alone, and lonely. Has he gotten in your way in the past few weeks?

1. Consider and discuss how Satan is trying to interfere with your attempts to connect.

2. What are your distractions? What have you done about them? What more will you do about them?

3. A participant told me that one of her friends complained, "You gave a gift to that person you don't even know, but you didn't give me one." How have you met with resistance from your friends? How have you handled criticism?

4. What do you think of the following replies to a criticism like the one above?

   a. "I don't want you to feel left out. I am trying to make others feel significant and feel connected. Would you like to go with me the next time I go?"

b. "Yes, I did give a gift to Tonya. I'm sorry you feel neglected because of that. I want you to know that any time I give you something, it is because I want to and not because I feel obligated."

c. Evaluate the pros and cons of responses "a" and "b."

Meditate: 1. To reflect on, ponder. 2. To plan or intend in the mind.

What are you thinking? We began this chapter with Philippians 4:8 which commands us to meditate positively. Are you thinking negatively and fearfully?

Have you resisted making connections because you are afraid the effort will demand a lot of time? Connections can be strong and deep without leading to the kind of relationship that demands a lot of time. You are not being asked to go out and make a new BFF (best friend forever).

Consider this allegory: I need to keep my fingers connected to my hand which is connected to my arm, etc., etc. Now that doesn't mean I have to spend my life checking on my fingers, but I need to be mindful of my fingers, to keep them out of harm's way and care for them, because they are important to the body.

Describe your failed attempts to connect, if any. How do you feel about them?

Evaluate your feelings of discouragement.

1. When did you begin to feel discouraged?

2. Have you been able to overcome these discouragements?

3. Where can a discouraged person find help, and how can that help be accessed?

Has any recipient reacted negatively? If so, describe the occurrence and tell how you feel about it.

Do you need to meet with the recipient about the matter? Do you need support? If so, who will you call for help?

What other methods has Satan used in an effort to stop you? (boredom, exhaustion, fear). Is it easier to resist Satan's wiles when you recognize them or when they slip up on you?

Consider and discuss your participation.

Describe your progress toward connection with someone.

Describe any increased understanding of yourself.

Describe or list any increased understanding of the people with whom you have connected.

Describe or list increased understanding of people in general.

Our number one fear is usually that of rejection. In our minds, people's reactions are a barometer of our worth. That fear can paralyze us.

The next time fear makes you hesitate, read Philippians 4:8 aloud, then try the following self-talk:

- "Rejection is not an indication of my worth. God has established my worth and has redeemed me by the blood of his Son!"

- "I might look foolish to some people. No doubt Jesus' washing the feet of his disciples looked foolish to some people. I will keep on trying to connect."

If fear kept you from following through on any of these assignments, name the assignment(s) and describe the conversation you had with yourself at the time.

If you are having difficulty *receiving* an offer of bonding, consider discussing this difficulty with a trustworthy friend or a professional.

The First Requirement

It takes two to form a bond. You, the reader, are taking the initiative, but you cannot do it alone. For there to be a connection, both of you have to give and receive. Let's evaluate your progress.

If you are meeting resistance in your attempts to connect, what will you do?

How will you respond when someone tries to connect with you?

How can you make it easier for the one trying to connect with you?

What is God's role in your efforts to connect with others?

Compare your efforts to connect with that of a gardener who plants a seed and then waits for rain and sunshine to moisten and warm the ground so the seed can germinate. The gardener can't uncover the seed every day to see what is happening, but she should know that she will have to water the seed if the rains don't come.

What can you do while you wait for the harvest of your efforts at friendship?

Here is a thought to keep you going:

Keep your life free from love of money, and be content with what you have, for he has said, "I will never leave you nor forsake you." So we can confidently say, "The Lord is my helper; I will not fear; what can man do to me?" (Hebrews 13:5–6).

Meditate and evaluate. Don't stop trying to connect with others.

Others

Lord help me live from day to day
In such a self-forgetful way
That even when I kneel to pray
My prayer shall be for—Others.

Help me in all the work I do
To ever be sincere and true,
And know that all I do for you
Must needs be done for—Others.

Let "self" be crucified and slain
And buried deep; and all in vain,
May efforts be to rise again
Unless to live for—Others.

And when my work on earth is done
And my new work in heaven's begun,
May I forget the crown I've won
While thinking still of—Others.

Others, Lord, yes others
Let this my motto be:
Help me to live for others
That I may live like Thee.

—Charles D. Meigs (written sometime between 1890 and 1902)

Jump into the Deep End

10

> Put on then, as God's chosen ones, holy and beloved, compassionate hearts, kindness, humility, meekness, and patience, bearing with one another and, if one has a complaint against another, forgiving each other; as the Lord has forgiven you, so you also must forgive (Colossians 3:12–13).

At one point, the church of Christ in Corinth was segmenting. Get it? They were disconnecting from each other. Members were choosing sides. They needed someone to stand up and say, "Hey, wait a minute. We are a body with connected members."

Oh, wait. Paul did that! Paul's first letter to the church at Corinth was written to confront the divisive issues and challenge the congregation to correct sinful behaviors. Paul didn't enjoy writing such a letter, but he loved them enough to say difficult things. We show our love by honestly, and even tearfully, sharing our concerns.

In the second letter to the Corinthians, Paul reassures them that his motives were out of love.

> And I wrote as I did, so that when I came I might not suffer pain from those who should have made me rejoice, for I felt sure of all of you, that my joy would be the joy of you all. For I wrote to you out of much affliction

and anguish of heart and with many tears, not to cause you pain but to let you know the abundant love that I have for you (2 Corinthians 2:3–4).

Visible and Valued

Jim McGuiggan said, "When God came, he came talking." He further said,

> If you take the time to look, you will find at least forty times that verses in the book of Mark show Jesus as teacher and preacher—using words to communicate with and connect with people, and by setting a perfect example. Then he sent his disciples out to do the same—preach and teach. I perceive preaching as done by someone, front-and-center, speaking words and not necessarily ever knowing if the listener understood, agreed with, or even assimilated the information. Teaching is much more than using words. A true teacher is an example. She appeals to all methods of learning by providing visuals, a format for the student to demonstrate understanding, and an opportunity for the student to practice.

Challenge: To summon to action, effort, or use.

Words are important, not only our choice of them but how we say them. By the proper selection and use of words, we can let others know they are visible and valued.

Jesus spoke to the Samaritan woman at the well in a confrontational way (John 4:7–26). He spoke to a woman in a time and culture when men did not speak to women who were strangers. He didn't hold back when talking about the man she was living with who was not her husband. He didn't hold back when he talked to her about the way she worshiped. Note that the confrontation dealt with important things—relationships and worship—rather than the trivial. Notice also that the Samaritan woman spoke to Jesus. A proper Samaritan lady probably would not have done so.

Jesus spoke bluntly in Matthew 23 when he called the scribes and Pharisees hypocrites and blind guides. He did not rudely vent his emotions, but he got their attention. Jesus spoke tenderly to the adulterous woman in John 8. He talked patiently to his disciples and the multitudes when they didn't understand his message. He spoke scathingly to the self-righteous (McGuiggan 105–111).

Perfect Response

In Luke 10:38–42 we find Jesus speaking honestly and lovingly to Martha, in whose home he was visiting. Martha was justifiably concerned about getting everything on the table, so she asked Jesus to tell her sister Mary to be more helpful. How would you have answered Martha? I probably would have tried to diffuse the tension without taking sides. Some might have chosen Martha's side because she was justified in her request. But Jesus defended Mary because she was listening to him. He responded to Martha in truth with much love and courage. He was honest and direct. He spoke to Martha about herself. He said what others already knew but wouldn't say. He spoke with just the right words and the right tone at the right time, and obviously, with just the right look on his face. He did it correctly.

The Deep End Can Be Cold

I often feel that I won't answer well when someone really needs to hear the truth. Consequently, I pretend I don't see what needs to be addressed. I am behaving like a coward, but I tell myself I am just being polite or non-judgmental. I hesitate or withdraw because I know that to speak up will make the relationship messy.

To speak up and say the thing that needs to be said requires that we care enough. It requires time to consider our choice of words and our motives. It requires that we risk something important (our relationship as it is) for something more important (helping someone choose a higher priority and the depth of relationship that can develop). It further requires that we be prepared to get involved, because there might be consequences. Truth isn't always accepted easily. It can be cold and lonely in the deep end.

Make two suggestions for speaking up in interest of another's soul. (See page 97.)

Gut Level Communication

Connections require communication. Deep connections involve gut-level and peak-level talking and listening. (See page 98 of this book.) Some people can easily jump into the deep end and share gut-level feelings. They have no difficulty telling others what they really think because they want to get it off their chest or because of their conviction that the other person needs to know in order to be a better person. Some people believe that speaking their mind will protect them from misunderstandings. These reasons have little or nothing to do with connecting with others. This kind of communication rarely deepens relationships.

If you choose to communicate with me by indiscriminately speaking your mind, what I learn is where your boundaries are. That's not always a bad thing, of course. If I respect your boundaries, I am less likely to anger you, and the chance of our becoming enemies is greatly reduced. But that does not necessarily deepen a relationship. Without love you are a clanging cymbal (1 Corinthians 13:1), and without love your confrontation will not deepen your connections. Although, perhaps, if I am open to truth or seeking to change, I will be able to hear and accept what you say in spite of your motives.

Here's an inspired example of Paul's gut-level communication:

For our appeal does not spring from error or impurity or any attempt to deceive, but just as we have been approved by God to be entrusted with the gospel, so we speak not to please man, but to please God who tests our hearts. For we never came with words of flattery, as you know, nor with a pretext for greed—God is witness. Nor did we seek glory from people, whether from you or from others, though we could have made demands as apostles of Christ. But we were gentle among you, like a nursing mother taking care of her own children. So, being affectionately desirous of you, we were ready to share with you not only the gospel of God but also our own selves, because you had become very dear to us (1 Thessalonians 2:3–8).

Note that Paul told the Thessalonians he not only shared the gospel but also himself. The deepest connections require just that, sharing ourselves. This thought strikes a personal chord with me.

Care and Show It

Recently I placed my membership with a local congregation because of a young Bible class teacher. She communicated with her ladies' class on a gut level, similar to the way Paul communicated with the Thessalonians. She shared herself, was transparent and caring, and invited the class to relate to her and to the message of the scripture they were discussing. I wanted to be a part of a church in which members share themselves.

Years ago there was a time in my life when I had a difficult time attending church services. I sometimes drove to worship, sat in my car on the parking lot, and cried. Then I cried all the way home. I know now I was grieving a tremendous loss, but at the time I was so overwhelmed with feelings that I couldn't name them. I often walked through the house with hands and eyes lifted upward, and all I could think was, "God. My Father. What? What?" For the first time in my life, talking to God was impossible. I only moaned. Words escaped me.

My dear friend Connie, for whom I had an appreciation at the time but not a really close friendship, deepened our connection by speaking to me in much the same way I think Jesus spoke to the woman at the well—lovingly and honestly. When I missed the assembly on Sunday, Connie called on Monday, each time with the same message: "I didn't see you yesterday. Were you there?"

"No."

"Are you sick?"

"No."

"Well, I just want you to know you were missed. I'll look for you next time."

Sometimes after phoning me, she sent a card. She never criticized; I don't think she ever tried to make me feel guilty. She just let me know she cared, week after week for about eighteen months, the amount of time it took me to get my balance and stand up again. Each time I was not in my place, Connie challenged me; she summoned me to action. She would not let me lie down and die. Because of her patience and steadfastness, I came to trust her. Then I began to open up and share myself in a way I had never done with anyone but God. I jumped into the deep end.

Notice the tone of love in the following verses:

> Not that we lord it over your faith, but we work with you for your joy, for you stand firm in your faith. For I made up my mind not to make another painful visit to you. For if I cause you pain, who is there to make me glad but the one whom I have pained? And I wrote as I did, so that when I came I might not suffer pain from those who should have made me rejoice, for I felt sure of all of you, that my joy would be the joy of you all. For I wrote to you out of much affliction and anguish of heart and with many tears, not to cause you pain but to let you know the abundant love that I have for you (2 Corinthians 1:24–2:4).

A Place for Me

During my time of grief, I did not lose my faith. I was still trust-ing God. But I did lose my place. Connie conveyed through her words and her tone of voice that I was important to her and to the body of Christ. She is the only one in a congregation of nearly a thousand who was brave enough to take a chance that I would believe her motives were right before God. Perhaps there were hundreds of others who prayed for me but were afraid to confront me. I am confident there were many who talked to each other about me: "Wonder what's going on with Doritta?" But none of them talked to me. Connie was my lifeline, and she persevered in the connection.

The 1 Thessalonians passage on page 133 reminds me of the saying, quoted very often in the '70s, and quoted earlier in this book: "People don't care how much you know until they know how much you care." Gut-level communication in order to deepen connections requires a high level of trust. You have to trust the other person, and the other person has to trust you.

Choose Your Adventure

This week's assignments are at gut level. Maybe you are not ready for gut-level communication with the people with whom you have initiated connections in the past few weeks. If your new connections have not reached this level, please don't use gut-level communication. Instead, consider deepening a relationship with someone you have known for some time and failed to progress past a superficial level. If you are not ready for gut-level commu-nication with anyone, don't allow yourself any negative feelings about not being ready. No guilt.

Before you panic, keep reading. The assignments do ask you to act on a deeper level but not to go to battle! Your choices for this week might be difficult, and you should feel at least a little apprehensive any time you share or invite gut-level communication. If not, check your motivation. But I believe you will be able to choose at least one of the tasks.

1. *Pray daily for a Christian who has been open about struggling with her daily walk.* Let her know you love her as she is, because God loves you as you are. This person may be waiting for someone to show support, so be ready. You might need to be available for a long time.

2. *Deepen your connection with a trustworthy person by sharing something that really matters to you or by asking about something that you know is burdensome for that person.* Always pray first, and always check your motivation.

3. *Choose someone who formerly has seemed distant.* Maybe it's someone you don't like. It might even be someone you have clashed with in the past. If so, seek an opportunity to discuss the situation. Has she wronged you? This is not about hurt feelings, but a wrong. Have you wronged her? If so, confess your error and ask forgiveness. Do all you can to make things right. If there is nothing to forgive her for, but you "just don't like her," take time to get to know her. If the person you don't like is going to heaven and you are going to heaven, guess what? You're going to be in heaven together. The reason that would happen is because God loves both of you, warts and all. Maybe you really can overlook the other person's warts, and maybe the other person will overlook your warts too.

4. *Comfort a grieving or discouraged person.* Keep in mind that no matter how long it has been since "the event," it continues to be a loss. Maybe you would have moved on by now, but we are not all alike. She is not you! We recuperate at different speeds. When you visit with someone who is discouraged, put aside any judgments about whether the cause is trivial or

deserving of attention. It is not up to you to fix it. You don't get to choose the amount of weight another person should be able to carry or how long the weight should be carried. Everyone has her limits.

5. *Do some people bring out the worst in you and help you to lose your patience? Choose such a person for this assignment.* Do her a good deed that comes from your heart—no pretending. For example, perhaps you are impatient around negative, whiny people. Remember, we are allowing others to be themselves. It's a fact: there are Eeyores in this life. Accept that and give to them sincerely. Pray about how you feel around this person—several times if you need to—and search the word for solutions from the Holy Spirit. Give this person a few minutes with your listening ear.

Before You Take Action

- Read and think about each option.
- Make a selection. You may choose one or more options.
- Think about why you selected that option.
- Why didn't you select the other option(s)?
- Pray and complete the task(s).

Sample Scene

Imagine yourself in the following situation. You do not have a deep connection with Martha, although you would like to develop one. An opportunity arises.

You: "Martha, remember door-knocking is this Saturday."

Martha: "I know door-knocking is this Saturday but I don't know if I am going. I went last month and someone slammed a door in my face. That felt awful. I wanted to go home and cry.

I don't know if I can take that again." (Martha has shared gut-level feelings with you. She has trusted you with these feelings. She is not proud of having given up, because she feels that some will judge her reaction unfairly. How you respond is important.)

You: "Martha, I had a similar experience. I know how it made me feel and it wasn't a good feeling." (By telling Martha you have had a similar experience, you deepen the connection. She now knows you understand. You also deepened the bond when you allowed her to express her feelings without preaching her a sermon such as "You shouldn't let rejection bother you, because, in so doing, you're giving up and making Satan happy!" Instead, you are remaining quiet and waiting. Your open-minded stance frees her from being controlled by your feelings. You refrain from telling her how she should feel. How do you think Martha will react to your concern?)

Martha: "Well, I guess I shouldn't let that stop me. How did you handle your situation?" (Don't be quick to talk. Apparently Martha is trusting you with her feelings. She is sharing on a gut level. The time is not right for a sermon.)

You: "I also thought about not trying again." (Now you are sharing on a gut level.)

 ## It's Your Turn

After you complete your assignment, share the changes you experienced in your life with the class. Caution! Never share the other person's story.

1. In the story above about you and Martha, if you both continue to talk, how might the conversation proceed, and how might it end?

2. Was this assignment more difficult for you than previous ones? Why or why not?

3. If you made an effort to deepen a connection, describe what you did and how you felt.

4. Did you remember to listen? What did you hear?

5. Describe what you learned about yourself that helps you understand who you are.

6. What did your experience teach you about what you value?

7. What did you do that showed how you valued the other person?

8. If the other person did not respond, what might that mean?

9. If there was a response, describe it here:

10. Did the other person reach out to you in return? If so, describe that here:

11. Was there an indication that the recipient felt supported or encouraged?

12. Did the other person reach out to you in return? If so, describe that here:

13. If you are comfortable, discuss in class or with a trustworthy friend your feelings about your role in this assignment. Do not discuss the subject of your confrontation or the other person's response. That is your contact's story, not yours. But discuss your feelings, motivation, and spiritual growth.

Talk to God about your efforts to deepen connections.

Avoid Faulty Connections

Count it all joy, my brothers, when you meet trials of various kinds, for you know that the testing of your faith produces steadfastness. And let steadfastness have its full effect, that you may be perfect and complete, lacking in nothing. If any of you lacks wisdom, let him ask God, who gives generously to all without reproach, and it will be given him (James 1:2–5).

You are almost three months into the process of forming bonds. Your continuing work proves your steadfastness. But are you getting bored? Tired of thinking about this subject? Ready to move on to something else? Want to stop spending so much time thinking about other people? I'm calling on you to persevere. Two more weeks. One more assignment and then we wrap it up. Can you do it? Will you?

🎵 *Retain and persevere.* "As for that in the good soil, they are those who, hearing the word, hold it fast in an honest and good heart, and bear fruit with patience" (Luke 8:15).

Are you producing a crop of connections? Are the results of your efforts during this study helping members of the body of Christ to recognize their significance? Are you recognizing your significance in the body? Are you producing a crop of understanding—understanding yourself and others?

🎵 *Seek the eternal.* "He will render to each one according to his works: to those who by patience in well-doing seek for glory and honor and immortality, he will give eternal life" (Romans 2:6–7).

We can work ourselves to a standstill in order to have a big house, the latest appliances, trendiest clothes and cars, and other things that don't last. Material things don't last and we can't take them with us and the people we leave behind will not remember what we owned. Only the things we do for each other will last beyond our lifetimes and be remembered by others.

🎵 *Want perseverance? Suffer.* "More than that, we rejoice in our sufferings, knowing that suffering produces endurance, and endurance produces character, and character produces hope" (Romans 5:3–4).

It is not easy to make and keep connections. It requires us to turn off electronics and dedicate some time to people. It requires us to leave our reserved seats in worship and cross the aisle to express love to our brothers and sisters. It sometimes requires planning ahead and preparing, and then time in the actual doing. It requires perseverance to show people they are significant.

I once saw a movie in which the character of a 12-year-old depicted rejection. He cried, "I am nothing! I am nothing!" This belief that he was worthless made him a target of manipulators who persuaded him to do hateful things. The hateful things he did, in turn, made him feel worthless.

Helping a person to break the cycle and see that he has value and significance will require perseverance from someone or many someones. Remember the poem we read in chapter 4 on page 71? People are afraid to believe they have value. We must persevere in making connections.

🎵 *Confidence—a keeper.* "Therefore do not throw away your confidence, which has a great reward. For you have need of endurance, so that when you have done the will of God you may receive what is promised" (Hebrews 10:35–36). The confidence spoken of here is the confidence to "draw near with a true heart" because of the blood of Christ (vv. 19–22).

While this passage is talking about steadfastness in the face of persecution, don't you find that your efforts to persevere in any area are rewarding in and of themselves? James 1:4 says, "And let steadfastness have its full effect, that you may be perfect and complete, lacking in nothing."

Do you sometimes feel you are lacking? Maybe it's because you are being tempted to quit something. Reflect on a difficult thing you have accomplished. Did it at first seem impossible? Did you seriously think about giving up? Perhaps you did give up for a season, but then you were recharged or received some support or advice and decided to continue trying. And, perhaps with your last ounce of strength, you finished the work. How did you feel? Strong? Capable? Smart? Able?

🎵 *Giving adds value.* "Let them thank the Lord for his steadfast love, for his wondrous works to the children of men!" (Psalm 107:8).

"We love because he first loved us" (1 John 4:19). Love gives. God loves us, and he gives to us. How can we receive and recognize God's unfailing love and not want to show our love in return by caring for his church?

We love because he first loved us. We need to nourish that love by recognizing it, thinking about it, being grateful for it, and sharing ourselves with others. Sharing our talents and skills places value on those talents and skills.

Sharing yourself with others places value on yourself and on the other person. For example, I crochet and knit and give away coasters, dishcloths, tea cozies, and other small gifts. I am only passably good at crocheting. I know my work is not as good as that of my friend Linda Gurganus. I place a low value on my skills. However, I love to do needlework, and I know that the best thing about any gift given to me is the message that someone thought of me. So I make and give. When I give my project to someone, I place a higher value on my skills. Sharing heaps value on yourself and others.

Develop a Steadfast Mindset

The word *steadfast* always reminds me of the book of Nehemiah. Read the names of individuals and families who took their places around the rubble that once fortified Jerusalem and notice that each did his part in rebuilding that wall (Nehemiah 3). Can you picture it? Put yourself there. You are working, doing your part. You look to your left; brother Jones is working. You look to your right; sister Smith is working. You look all around; people are in place doing their jobs. Makes you want to continue to do your job, doesn't it?

What if you look to the left and brother Jones has decided to go home and work on his house? Then you look to your right and sister Smith is taking a nap or texting a friend. Or what if you decide to leave because you want a bigger house and don't see how working on the city wall is more important than providing for your family? Think about the effect. Years ago, Barb Cox, a woman with a debilitating muscular disease, was always present for worship. She paid dearly to be there. Her steadfastness had a huge impact on me and others in the congregation.

Your brothers and sisters will see your commitment to them, and your steadfastness will produce hope!

Choose Your Adventure

1. Call on others who have the same appreciation for a mutual friend who shows steadfastness. Take the steadfast friend out to dinner and sing, "For She's a Jolly Good Fellow."

2. Offer to help a steadfast teacher make visuals for a 13-week quarter. Tell her you are using this means to express gratitude for her steadfastness.

3. Choose someone who is steadfast, dependable, and committed. Let her know by card, phone, or gift that you appreciate her qualities. Remind her of the security she can find in God. You may use the Bible verses in this chapter, as well as myriads of others you can find in God's word.

4. By now you are probably finding your own opportunities for connection during your personal and family weekly activities. You don't need my suggestions. What can you do this week to show those you naturally interact with that you have a steadfast appreciation for them?

Steadfastness: Constancy, endurance; in the New Testament the characteristic of a man who is not swerved from his deliberate purpose and his loyalty to faith and piety by even the greatest trials and sufferings; patient, steadfast; a patient, steadfast waiting for; a patient enduring, sustaining, perseverance.

Before You Take Action

- Read and think about each option.

- Make a selection. You probably began this study by selecting options suggested by me, but as your confidence builds, you will develop your own.

What attracted you to the option you chose? Write your answer and then tell why you did not select a different option.

Pray and complete the task(s), then answer these questions.

1. Luke 8:15 teaches that perseverance (patience) will produce a crop. Write the name of a steadfast acquaintance. List the accomplishments of that person as a result of perseverance.

2. How are you applying Romans 5:3–4 in your efforts to connect with others? How can these two verses help you to avoid faulty connections?

3. Describe how steadfastness in someone you know produced character and hope.

4. What changes in your attitude about your connections have occurred since you began this study?

5. What skills are you improving through your steadfast commitment to connection? What pitfalls have you learned to avoid?

6. When you commended someone for steadfastness, what response did you receive?

7. What effect did it have on you to spend time thinking about someone else's perseverance? What effect did it have on you to express your appreciation?

8. Think about how God has shown steadfast, unfailing love to you. God inhabits praise, being "enthroned on the praises of Israel" (Psalm 22:3). Close your eyes and spend some time praising him for his steadfast, unfailing love. Name some of the ways he has proven himself to be steadfast in your life.

9. T. Pierce Brown, a well-known gospel preacher, once said, "The gospel is the power of God to save, and if one gets his power and utterance from the Holy Spirit, and is strengthened by the Spirit in the inner man (Ephesians 3:16), the

chances of his burning out would be almost non-existent."
How do you feel about his statement?

Talk to God about your steadfastness or your need to develop
steadfastness to avoid faulty connections.

Plug into the Main Power Source

12

The God who made the world and everything in it, being Lord of heaven and earth, does not live in temples made by man, nor is he served by human hands, as though he needed anything, since he himself gives to all mankind life and breath and everything. And he made from one man every nation of mankind to live on all the face of the earth, having determined allotted periods and the boundaries of their dwelling place, that they should seek God, and perhaps feel their way toward him and find him. Yet he is actually not far from each one of us, for "In him we live and move and have our being"; as even some of your own poets have said, "For we are indeed his offspring" (Acts 17:24–28).

For his invisible attributes, namely, his eternal power and divine nature, have been clearly perceived, ever since the creation of the world, in the things that have been made (Romans 1:20).

Not that I have already obtained it or have already become perfect, but I press on so that I may lay hold of that for which also I was laid hold of by Christ Jesus . . . I do not regard myself as having laid hold of it yet; but one thing I do: forgetting what lies behind and reaching forward to what lies ahead, I press on toward the goal for the prize of the upward call of God in Christ Jesus.

... Let us keep living by that same standard to which we have attained ... join in following my example, and observe those who walk according to the pattern you have in us. ...

For our citizenship is in heaven, from which also we eagerly wait for a Savior, the Lord Jesus Christ; who will transform the body of our humble state into conformity with the body of his glory, by the exertion of the power that he has even to subject all things to himself (Philippians 3:12–14, 16–17, 20–21 NASB).

What do you know about heaven that makes you want to be there? Stop reading for about thirty seconds and write a few of the reasons in the margin—not a comprehensive list; just a few things. If your list includes "to be with God," take thirty seconds more to list a few of the reasons you want to be with God. What do you know about him that makes you want to be with him? I ask these questions to provoke you to think about your motivation. Do you want to go to heaven and be with God because someone said you should, because you don't want to go to the other place, or because you have learned so much about God you can hardly wait to walk and talk with him the way Adam and Eve did in the Garden of Eden?

🎵 "Do two walk together, unless they have agreed to meet?" (Amos 3:3).

🎵 "Enoch walked with God after he fathered Methuselah 300 years and had other sons and daughters" (Genesis 5:22).

Altogether Enoch lived 365 years, he walked with God. Then he was no more, because God took him away. Three hundred sixty-five years! God wanted to be with Enoch, and Enoch wanted to be with God. Enoch walked with God, and God took him away. Do you enjoy God's company? Does God enjoy your company?

Your Power Source

Why do you enjoy associating with certain people? Envision associating with a favorite friend. Quickly jot down a few reasons you enjoy her company. How do you know these reasons? Through experiences and communication, right? How often do you want to be with your favorite person? How often do you talk to your favorite person? We make time to talk to those we love. And we are interested in their opinions and ideas. It is that concept and more that permeates our relationship with God. The more we know about God, the more we want to be with him.

Every minute we draw breath, we have the gift of God's presence. He's there, waiting for us to communicate with him. He gave us the word to communicate his will to us. He also communicates with us every day in the way he cares for us. Do you talk to him?

> God hears his name constantly blasphemed by the world. When his children call his name, his "aching ears are soothed" (Young 203).

In prayer, I talk to God. I have the right and the duty to come boldly or "with confidence draw near" (Hebrews 4:16), and he wants me to "continue steadfastly in prayer, being watchful in it with thanksgiving" (Colossians 4:2). Are you listening and talking to God? Does your relationship with God go both ways?

Make a quick search on "prayers of the Bible," such as those of David, Solomon, Jehoshaphat, and Hezekiah. Choose your favorite, and read it first thing every morning for a week. Share your results with the class.

What do you know about God that makes you want to be with him? His character, of course. But those who do not know him cannot know his character. How often do you talk to God? How often do you let him talk with you by reading his word? Are you interested in God—really interested in who he is and what matters to him? We don't have any great desire to be with someone we don't know anything about. As we get to know another person, we discover things that connect us to each other. It is that way in our connection with God.

Become aware that the Bible is your way to God. As you study his word daily, look for descriptions that paint his character. Begin your own list, perhaps in the back of your study Bible. Here are a few to get you started:

Numbers 23:19_____

Deuteronomy 4:31_____

2 Samuel 22:32-34_____

John 4:24_____

Spend some time reading Psalms, considering the names of God used there. Make a list of at least three of the names and provide references.

Trust God's Power

The Israelites saw God's power in how they were released from slavery, saved at the Red Sea, provided food and water in the wilderness, and saved many other times in many other ways while they traveled toward the land God had promised them.

God communicated with them all the way. They lived these facts, so surely they had them in their head. Right? And yet they complained and whined all the way, continuously asking God for more. The four books of Exodus through Deuteronomy are filled with examples.

Did any of the Israelites have a deep connection with God? Yes, a few, Moses, Joshua, and Caleb among them. How do you know they had a deep connection with God? We know because their behavior demonstrated a complete trust in God. He spoke, and they obeyed.

Fast forward about forty years. The Israelites are ready to take Canaan. Jericho was first on the agenda. Rahab, a Canaanite, had not experienced God's almighty works, but she had heard of them (Joshua 2:10–11). When the time came for her to choose whose side she was on, she trusted and obeyed the God of the universe. The difference between the whining, complaining Israelites and the trusting, obedient Rahab is that, while both had the facts in their heads, only one had them in her heart as well.

Circle the phrase that depicts your connection with the Power Source.

- Connected to God for the things he can give you or do for you.

- Connected to God because you have come to trust and obey him.

Talk to someone who is knowledgeable about the difference between a 220-volt and a 110-volt electrical outlet. Compare your findings to your spiritual connection to God. How is it possible to limit your companionship with God? How will you expand your capacity for Power?

We deepen our connections with humans by sharing ourselves with each other on a gut level. How does one deepen a connection with God Almighty? Think some more about Rahab. What effect do you think it had on her when she endangered her life by aligning herself with God? There is nothing shallow in that choice. Seems like gut-level to me. From Joshua 6:17, do you think Rahab's connection with God was deepened when her trust was validated? Does believing facts initiate a connection? Maybe.

Consider the first generation of Israelites coming out of Egyptian slavery. Even if we give them the benefit of the doubt and say they believed the facts, it did not lead to faith in God. Remember, the definition of *faith* is compound—to trust and obey. Faith is not trust only or obedience only. Faith is trust and obedience. The Israelites had the care of the God of the universe, and all they seemed to do was whine and complain and lose their lives in the wilderness. Rahab trusted and obeyed and was saved. Connection was initiated when she heard and believed the far-reaching news of God's miracles. The connection became stronger and deeper when she trusted and obeyed.

We talked about being connected to God in chapter 2. We looked at Bible verses that show us he wants us to choose to be connected to him. If you have chosen to be connected to God, is that connection deeper now than at first? Is it deeper than it was last year? Deeper than ten years ago? If so, how did that happen? If not, I pray you will think about that soon.

What have you done to deepen your connection with God?
Write about that here:

When the above question was asked in a ladies' Bible class, the women responded in the following categories: music, nature, and fasting.

Music

Several of the women described how Christian music changes hearts, draws people toward God, and even deepens the connection with God. William Congreve, in his play, "The Mourning Bride," written in 1697, said that "musick [sic] has charms to soothe a savage breast." How do you feel when you pop in a CD of hymns and spiritual songs and really listen to the words? Have you physically and emotionally responded when words and melody have combined to send a powerful message about God? Are there times when the message speaks to you so powerfully it makes you want to change your behavior? Yeah. Like that. Music can deepen one's connection with God.

Nature

Other women in the class talked about how nature reminds them of God's great power and strengthens their confidence in a God who can create the majestic and the common. How about you? Are you affected when the sand caresses your feet as the ocean waves roll in and gently wash them or as you gaze down into the vastness of the Grand Canyon? How about as you look up at the trees of California's majestic Redwood Forest, Zambia's and Zimbabwe's Victoria Falls, or Cape Town's Table Mountain? Or are you most affected when you sit quietly in your backyard listening to the birds sing, watching a hummingbird, or watching and listening to a powerful thunderstorm or a gentle rain? What happens when you spend five minutes praising God for his creation? Remember, God inhabits praise (Psalm 22:3). Be there.

Change of Environment

Class participant Pam Lentz says working at summer youth camp makes her more aware of scripture. She sometimes can hear a Bible message similar to those she has heard all her life, but while sitting among hundreds of young people, the perspective is different. The effect of the message is often more powerful than usual. She recommends ladies' retreats for the same reason.

Similarly, Ann Dunaway says that when she studies with a small group that is seeking truth about a specific subject, she is drawn nearer to God. The focus is different and so is the perspective when you are listening in different environments. When you want a deeper connection with God, don't limit your time with him to Sunday worship and personal studies. Look for God in different places, at different times, and with different people.

Reproach: Taunt of enemy; condition of shame, disgrace.

Fasting

Have you considered fasting as a way to deepen your connection with God? "What?" you say. "Fast? Christians don't fast." It's true we are not commanded to fast, but fasting was practiced in the early church (cf. Acts 13:1–3; 14:21–23). Luke 4:1–19 tells us that Jesus fasted. And Jesus assumed his followers would fast. In Matthew 6:16, he said, "When you fast," not "if you fast." We heed Christ's comments in this passage about alms and praying but want to throw out his instructions about fasting. We want our three meals a day—and snacks. Furthermore, we want them supersized. Society today advocates that it is our right, even our need, to satisfy every human appetite. We want what we want when we want it.

The first time someone suggested fasting to me, I had been back in the States about two years after a six-year work in South Africa. While I was gone, my three sisters, with whom I had been very close while growing up, had continued to bond with each other. I had a hard time getting back into what I thought was my place in the circle. I felt like an outsider. I shared this with a friend at a young adult devotional. He asked me if I had fasted about it. "What?" I said. "Fast? No. What are you talking about?" And so I learned about fasting.

Do your own research about fasting. Write a basic outline below, with a note about health concerns.

In scripture, fasting is abstaining from food for spiritual purposes. It is done in order to direct one's thoughts toward God. During a fast, hunger reminds you that attachments to food and other things of this world do not control you. Fasting reminds you that God is more important than food. In the Bible, fasting was practiced in order to proclaim dependence on God rather than on earthly provisions.

In the Old Testament, fasting was commanded as a once-yearly event in Israel, *Yom Kippur*, which we know as the Day of Atonement. This fast included men, women, and children. On other occasions, fasting was not commanded but practiced at important events, most commonly for personal or public repentance and in seeking God's direction or his help.

From these references, find comments that clarify fasting:

> Psalm 35:13-14
>
> Psalm 69:10
>
> Daniel 9:1-3; 10:2-5
>
> Esther 4:3

Don't fast to change God. Don't do it to gain favor, twist his arm, barter, or bypass obedience. God is the same forever. Man is the one in need of change. Fasting changes you. It humbles you, subdues the flesh, disciplines you, brings peace, and gives you spiritual strength. In Psalm 69:10 David said he wept and humbled his soul with fasting. If we focus on the purpose of our fast, any deserved rebuke will surface.

Fasting reveals the things that control us. Often we use food to cover up or divert our attention when confronted by our deeper struggles. When we are unhappy or uncomfortable about ourselves, we often raid the refrigerator.

Fasting helps us keep a balance:

Fill in the blanks:

1 Corinthians 6:12, "'All things are lawful for me,' but not all things are _____. 'All things are lawful for me,' but I will not be _____ by anything."

1 Corinthians 9:27, "But I _____ my body and _____, lest after preaching to others I myself should be _____."

Romans 14:17, "For the kingdom of God is not a matter of _____ and _____ but of righteousness and peace and joy in the Holy Spirit."

In prayer and fasting, we talk and we listen. Realizing that God already knows everything sets us free to talk to him about the things we hide from everyone else and sometimes even from ourselves. Personally, when I fast I hear my own conscience confronting me about my behaviors, my doubts, and my attitudes, and reminding me that nothing is more important than my relationship with God.

Here is the rest of my story about fasting for my relationship with my sisters. For three days every time I thought about food I denied myself and said, "I want a close relationship with my sisters, without tearing up the relationship they have with each other. However, nothing is more important than my relationship with you, God." For two days, and maybe a little more, I said aloud, "I want *this.*" "Allow me *this.*" "Nevertheless, I want you more." By the third day I had stopped saying, "Give me *this*" and began being grateful to be back in the States where I could see and be with my sisters. I began to question myself: "What are you really asking for? What do you want changed?" A rebuke surfaced. I started my fast with a desire to recreate my role as "big sister" to my "little sisters." But my little sisters were now grown. My fasting changed me.

Shortly after my fast we all met at my Aunt Mary's house for Labor Day weekend. I think the focus of the fast—denying myself and what I wanted—helped me to let go of wanting "my place." This set me free to find joy in seeing their closeness with each other, which was a treasure within itself. Also it set me free from seeking my old place so I could find my new place in the circle.

Over the years I have learned that God can be trusted. With each trouble he helped me through, I have grown closer to him. But nothing draws me closer than denying myself food in order to show myself and God that he is the most important one in my life.

Reflect on a "trouble" you have experienced. How might fasting have helped you persevere? Why is fasting so often coupled with prayer?

Fasting is denying oneself. The fasting God prefers is described in Isaiah 58. Israel was using fasting to try to obligate or blackmail God and, at the same time, to present their "righteousness" to others. Isaiah tells us that God prefers a different kind of fasting. He prefers that we deny ourselves the right to sit on the couch and eat bonbons as often as we can afford it. He prefers fasting that shares the bonbons and the couch, one that shares what we have with others. God prefers fasting that gets us up off the couch and, either in our houses or outside them, shows God's love to others. Isaiah 58 is a powerful call to see other people, where they are and what they need, and share ourselves with them.

Read Isaiah 58 aloud. Which verse do you find to be the most moving? Write it here:

Choose Your Adventure

Here are your options:

1. *If you are not walking in agreement with God, pray daily about what is hindering you.* Begin walking after God (as in, "I'm going after something"); before God (meaning, in his sight, before his face); and with God, but not ahead of him (as Sarai

did in Genesis 16). Don't lag behind God, as Lot's wife did (Genesis 19). Describe here what is hindering your walk with him.

2. *Read 1 John.* Make a list of the things John says we may "know." How does this knowledge affect your confidence in God and your life with him as your leader?

3. *Create and laminate a note card of verses that will help some-one know how to come into agreement with God.* You may ask for help from your minister, an elder, an evangelist, or a member of your congregation who has a zeal for bringing the lost to the Lord. Review the card often. Keep in mind that on a daily basis we rarely are able to start at the top of the card and work our way through to the end when sharing the salvation story with someone. But if you are confident of what you know, you will be able to start where the door opens and "preach Jesus" as Philip did to the Ethiopian nobleman in Acts 8:26–39.

4. *Read the examples of obedience and salvation found in the book of Acts.*

   a. Acts 2

   b. Acts 8:12–13, 26–39

   c. Acts 9:1–19; 21:40–22:16; 26:1–32

   d. Acts 10

   e. Acts 13:13–48

   f. Acts 16:13–15

   g. Acts 16:22–34

   h. Acts 17:11–12

   i. Acts 17:16–34

   j. Acts 18:7–8

5. *Make a list of your favorite Christian songs, with a comment about each that makes it a favorite.*

6. *Spend at least five uninterrupted minutes every day this week telling God why you are grateful.*

7. *Read more about fasting and, if your health permits, commit to a 24-hour period of abstaining from solid food.* If your health does not permit a food fast, choose something else in your life that seems to dominate you: television, computer, or chocolate. Every time you begin to desire that thing you "must have," remind yourself that nothing is more important than your relationship with God. While doing without that "thing," pray about a personal struggle, a personal relationship, or any one thing that seems to be hindering a deep relationship with God. Don't fast about several things. Choose one thing.

Before You Take Action

🎵 Read and think about each of the options listed in "Choose Your Adventure."

🎵 Note that each option is inviting you to give serious thought about your connection to God. Does it really exist? If so, how deep is it?

🎵 Circle one or more selections.

🎵 Tell why you selected as you did. This is my final reminder that thinking about the "why" of our choices helps you understand yourself. Reasoning about your choices demonstrates your mindfulness. You are living with intention. Don't just let life happen to you. Make deliberate, prayerful choices.

🎵 Tell why you did not select the other option(s).

 Pray, complete your assignment, and then answer the following questions.

What do you think about these options? How do you feel about your selection?

If you fasted, describe the changes in your thoughts, feelings, and attitudes during the fast.

How are your choices relative to connection to God?

What long-range effect will your choice have in your life?

How will you use what you have done for this assignment in the future?

Do you have another idea for connecting with God? If so, describe it here and share your idea with others.

Talk to God about your relationship with him right now. Close your eyes, or open your eyes.

Describe aloud your relationship with him. How do you feel about that?

Does this moment provide you with an opportunity to recognize that your relationship with God is deeper than it was last year or ten years ago Describe.

What changes do you need to make? Don't kid yourself! There will always be self-corrections to make.

Tell God what changes you will make today in order to deepen your connection with him.

13

Welcome Ties that Bind!

According to legend found in the early church writings, the Apostle John was released from exile in Patmos and travelled from congregation to congregation appointing elders. In one unnamed congregation, John noticed a young man, powerful and full of energy. John charged an elder, "I commit this boy to you before the church and with Christ as witness. This is a charge to be taken seriously."

The elder not only accepted the charge, but also took the boy home with him, loved him, reared him, and eventually baptized him. Unfortunately, the elder didn't continue his diligent care of the young man—perhaps thinking that now that the youth had chosen to follow Jesus he would continue to make right choices by himself. But the young man drifted into the company of idle and reckless delinquents. He eventually became the leader of a gang of thieves.

Some years passed before John returned, and when he did he asked the elder for "the deposit which I and the Savior committed to you." The elder, having by this time forgotten the young man and his commitment, was at a loss, thinking John must be talking about a deposit of money! But there had been no money left with him.

John could see the confusion on the elder's face and demanded, "The boy! Where is the soul of my brother?" The elder broke into tears.

"He's dead."

"Dead? How did he die?" asked John.

"He is dead to God," the elder replied. "He turned wicked and left the church."

John was furious. "A fine guard of a brother's soul you are!"

John wasted no time, but immediately started searching for the young man. When John found him, the "thief" recognized John and started running away. John gave chase, shouting for him to stop running and come back with him. Picture the old man John, chasing the scared, young man. John would not give up. He continued to plead, eventually persuading the "thief" that Jesus would forgive.

The young man repented with tears and returned with John.

As we draw to the end of our study, let us return to the starting place. To begin with, connecting with others requires that we be able to see them. We have to develop eyes that will see others. Jesus saw souls:

- Beside a well

- In a tree

- Beside a pool

Beside a Well

John 4 tells of Jesus' talking with a Samaritan woman at Jacob's well in Sychar. How wonderful that they had uninterrupted time to talk about important things. In a time when respectful men didn't initiate conversations with respectable women, Jesus ignored customs so he could engage the woman in a soul-saving conversation.

In a Tree

Luke 19:1–10 tells of Jesus, looking above the crowd surrounding him and seeing someone who sought connection so desperately that he "ran on ahead and climbed up into a sycamore tree to see him," not caring that such behavior was very undignified for a grown man. Jesus looked above the heads of the crowd, made eye contact with Zacchaeus, and said, *Come down; let's have a conversation.* (Paraphrase mine.) We need to see the undignified, the unlovely.

Beside a Pool

All of us want to be seen—to know that we are not invisible. Imagine how the invalid in John 5 felt. There he lay by the Bethesda pool, one of many invalids waiting for healing in the waters. Jesus saw him and chose to connect with him instead of all the others in the crowd.

Practice Seeing Souls

We need to see people:

- In a restaurant
- In a classroom
- Across the aisle

Don't look only in the obvious places. Look high and low. And don't look just to connect with lovely people. Make a mindful decision to observe the people around you. See them as they are.

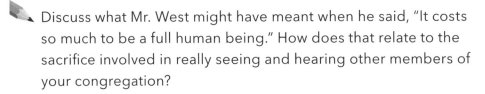

Charge: To entrust with a responsibility, duty, or obligation.

Learn to recognize that everyone, no matter how "pulled together" they may seem, is dealing with or compensating for something difficult in their lives. Act on the precept that sometimes just being recognized as a human being can help someone choose not to give up. Prayerfully and deliberately decide to see other people as they are.

It costs so much to be a full human being that there are very few who have the enlightenment or the courage, to pay the price . . . One has to abandon altogether the search for security, and reach out to the risk of living with both arms. One has to embrace the world like a lover. One has to accept pain as a condition of existence. One has to court doubt and darkness as the cost of knowing. One needs a will stubborn in conflict, but apt always to total acceptance of every consequence of living and dying (West).

 Discuss what Mr. West might have meant when he said, "It costs so much to be a full human being." How does that relate to the sacrifice involved in really seeing and hearing other members of your congregation?

It's Your Turn

 What was your favorite assignment during this course of study? Why?

How many connections have you begun as a result of participating in these assignments? Name them.

What will you do this week and in the future to maintain at least one of the connections you have made?

How have the class discussions helped you understand yourself and others and the process of connecting with others? Have they helped you disentangle your thoughts?

How have the class discussions helped you to have more confidence in reaching out to others?

Write out a Bible verse that relates to God's thoughts about connectedness. Cite the reference.

Write out a passage of scripture describing connection among believers. Remember to cite the reference.

> Becoming connected involves a transfer. Something real and actual changes hands, or in this case, hearts . . . you must receive the connection in order to make the transfer complete (Townsend 72).

Don't be afraid, timid, or hesitant to receive.

Don't Deny Your Design

You have been asked to initiate friendship, but both you and the recipient have to receive wholeheartedly for there to be a bond. The interaction of two people is required. It is risky, but oh so worth it. Besides, God designed us to be as close as a foot and toes.

What are you going to do with the connections you have made during this study? Nurture them? Drop them? It takes much time and energy to cement connections. You know that from your experiences of starting at a new school, in your courtship, in your marriage, or in your experiences in a civic organization. The more time and conversation you have with someone, the more you can know, understand, and accept that person; and the more you know about yourself. As the old song goes, "The more we get together, together, together; the more we get together, the happier we'll be."

If you are using this book for a class book, your final session should include time for discussion of your results and future goals. If you are using the book personally and singly, please spend time talking to God about the results of your efforts to connect with others. You have started something; something has been set in motion. If you have been genuine in your efforts and if you have been praying about the connections, God is working with you. He is all about relationships. He wants us to be connected, to have relationships, with him and with others. Don't stop just because you have finished this study. Continue to need connectedness, to ask for connections, and to receive connections.

You are a piece of the puzzle of someone else's life. You may never know where you fit, but others will fill the holes in their lives with pieces of you.
—Bonnie Arbon

I have a lump in my throat as I type these last few words. Dear reader, I pray you will work faithfully, lovingly, and patiently because God will see to it that your work bears fruit:

[Remember] before our God and Father your work of faith and labor of love and steadfastness of hope in our Lord Jesus Christ (1 Thessalonians 1:3).

Let steadfastness have its full effect, that you may be perfect and complete, lacking in nothing (James 1:4).

I am sure of this, that he who began a good work in you will bring it to completion at the day of Jesus Christ (Philippians 1:6).

Works Cited

Arrendondo, David E. Video online (You Tube), "Human Connectedness."

Bonhoeffer, Dietrich. *Life Together.* New York: Harper and Row, 1954. Print.

McGuiggan, Jim. *The God of the Towel.* Lubbock TX: Mantex Publishing Co., 1984. Print.

Young, Sarah. *Jesus Calling.* Nashville: Thomas Nelson, 1973. Print.

Thornton, W. Randolph. "Through Groups to God." *International Journal of Religious Education, 33,* April 1957. Print.

Townsend, John. *Loving People: How to Love and Be Loved.* Nashville: Thomas Nelson, 2010. Print.

West, Morris. *The Shoes of the Fisherman.* Toby Press, 2003. Print.